MEDITERRANEO
EDITIONS

SANTORINI

Text by
Tina Zisimou

Additional texts
Stella Kalogeraki

Photos - Layout
Vangelis Papiomytoglou

DTP
Natassa Antonaki

Translation
Jill Pittinger

© Copyright 2010
MEDITERRANEO EDITIONS
36 Govatzidaki str.
74100 Rethymno
tel. +30 28310 21590, fax +30 28310 21591
info@mediterraneo.gr
www.mediterraneo.gr

ISBN: 978-960-6848-36-0

SANTORINI

A GUIDE TO THE MOST BEAUTIFUL ISLAND IN THE WORLD

CONTENTS

INTRODUCTION

"You rose up out of the entrails of a thunderstorm..."

This is how Odysseus Elytis, the great Greek poet and winner of the Nobel Prize for Literature, describes the birth of of Santorini in his work 'Orientations, Ode to Santorini'.

The Byzantine chronicler Theophanes called it the 'island of the devil' and the traveller Sauger 'the island of demons'. Cursed by the gods but loved by humanity, with a natural landscape which combines awesome majesty and harsh ruggedness on its western shore with gentle tranquility and calm on its eastern shore, Santorini is an island of tremendous contrasts. It is a place where you can feel the tremors of the volcano which still simmers in its entrails, reserving for it a fate we cannot begin to imagine. It is therefore by no means strange that the feelings Santorini provokes in its visitors are also contradictory. There cannot be many other places in the whole world which are so repelling, and yet have so many fanatical devotees.

THE PLACE

GEOGRAPHY

Santorini (as Thera is popu-
larly known) lies in the
southern Aegean Sea
and is the southern-
most island of the Cyc-
lades (latitude 36° 22´ 3´´
N, longitude 25° 25´ 30´´ E).
It is 134 nautical miles from
Piraeus and 68 nautical miles
from Heraklion on Crete.
Together with its outlying
islands of Therasia, Palea and
Nea Kammeni, and Aspronisi
it forms the complex of
volcanic islands which is
internationally known to
geologists and volcanologists
as Santorini. The main island
has the shape of a half-moon,
with a length of around 18
km and a width that varies
between 2 and 6 km; its total
area is 73 sq km. The shore-
line perimeter is 36 nautical
miles long. The western side
of the island consists of steep
cliffs which reach a height
of 385 metres and plunge
to a similar depth below sea
level; the eastern shore is
low-lying and level, amenable
to the cultivation on terraces
that is a characteristic of all
of the Cycladic islands, and
there are a number of sandy
beaches. The highest mountain ridge is Mesa Vouno,
with its peak of Profitis Ilias
(565m). The climate does not
differ from that of the other
Cycladic islands. The winters
are gentle, with temperatures
between 6° and 10° C, and
snow is extremely rare. In
summer, the temperatures
are high, but the extreme

heat is tempered by the dry
atmosphere and the strong
north winds which frequently
blow over the whole of the
Aegean. There is very little
rainfall, only in winter, with
the result that the island is
arid; there are no springs or
streams.

The temperate climate and
the soil, which because of its
volcanic origin is very fer-
tile, make the island an ideal
place for the cultivation of a
number of crops. However,
the strong winds do not suit
the development of trees and
the lack of water limits agricultural production to a few
types of grain (mostly barley),
pulses (the local *fava* is well-
known), vegetables (the delicious, tiny island tomatoes are
unique of their kind, as well as
the white aubergines, ridged
cucumbers and the little
round courgettes), and grapes
for wine. The cultivation of
vineyards, which was already
carried on in antiquity, has

Wine and the little tomatoes of Santorini. Together with *fava*, these are the most representative agricultural products of the island.

particularly advanced in recent years and resulted in the production of wines which are acknowledged on the world markets.

Apart from its agricultural products, Santorini also exports Theran earth, a volcanic material that belongs to the category of pozzuolana but is extremely rich in silicic acid and low in calcium. Its composition makes it especially suitable for the production of hydraulic mortar, and for this reason it has been used for the construction of large underwater projects such as the harbours of Piraeus, Patras, Syros, Nafplion, Trieste and Alexandria, as well as for the Suez Canal.

Fossilised palm leaves.

Right: The crocus of the wall-paintings from Akrotiri (*Crocus cartwrightianus*).

THE LANDSCAPE AS IT ONCE WAS, AND AS IT IS NOW

The wall-paintings from Akrotiri tell us of a rich natural world, almost a paradise. Lilies, crocuses, sea daffodils and palm trees dominate in the pictures together with a plethora of wild animals such as ducks, monkeys, antelopes and deer, suggesting an almost obsessive relationship of the prehistoric inhabitants of Thera with Nature. The jewellery of the 'Potnia Theron' ('Mistress of the Animals'), who is Mother Nature herself, consists of ducks and dragonflies, while her clothing is decorated with rows of crocuses. Even if these pictures represent a fantasy world, the natural landscape of Santorini must have been richer before the volcanic eruption. Today, despite the unparalleled and impressive picture presented by the island - or rather the islands - the natural landscape is poor. With the exception of a few carobs and figs and solitary instances of other species, there are no large trees. Phrygana is the predominant type of vegetation, interspersed at Akrotiri with a few *Crocus cartwrightianus* which still grow there; this clearly indicates to us which species of the flower was collected by the female saffron-gatherers in the wall-paintings. Nevertheless, despite the apparent poverty of the flora, the actual number of species that have been recorded exceeds 600; this reflects the richness of the Greek flora in general. There are quite a few species of birds to be observed on the island. For example there are sea birds such as the silver gull (*Larus cachinans*) and Cory's shearwater (*Calonectris diomedea*), and also birds of prey such as the peregrine falcon (*Falco peregrinus*), Eleonora's falcon (*Falco eleonorae*), the kestrel (*Falco tinnunculus*), and Scops owl (*Athene noctua*). Small birds are everywhere to be seen

Cory's shearwater (*Calonectris diomedea*).

on the island, and on a walk from Fira to Imerovigli it is possible to spot the crag martin (*Ptyonoprogne rupestris*) on the steep walls of the caldera, and the willow warbler (*Phylloscopus trochilus*) rapidly flying from bush to bush, leaving snatches of its sweet warbled song in its wake.

The sea stock (*Matthiola sinuata*).

THE VINEYARD OF SANTORINI

Of the traditional products of Santorini, the most important for the economy of the island is wine. 75% of the 25,000 stremmata of land suitable for cultivation on the island is given over to vineyards.

Archaeological finds from the island attest to the cultivation of the grape during the 2nd millenium BC. Carbonised grape seeds identified amongst archaeobotanical remains and the clay treading floor found in the prehistoric settlement of Akrotiri indicate that wine was produced at that time. It is most probable that the wine was stored in the large spouted pithoi which were found in houses at the settlement. The ideogram for wine has been identified in an inscription in the Linear A script used by the inhabitants in the Minoan period.

The varieties of grapes grown on the island have remained the same for centuries, since Santorini has been lucky and not plagued by the phylloxera which destroyed huge expanses of vineyards in the rest of the world. Its sandy soils, lacking in nutrient substances and with a minimal clay content, have afforded protection from the disease; thus Santorini today constitutes one of the few areas of Europe in which self-rooting vines are grown. Of the around 40 indigenous varieties which still grow on the island, the most important are Asyrtiko, Aïdani, Atheri, Mantilaria, Potamisi, and Mavrotragano. The average yield per stremma (1,000 sq m) is low, around 350 kilograms, giving a total production of around 4,500 tonnes of grapes and 3,200 tonnes of wine which is, however, of the highest quality.

The most well-known wines of the island are the white dry 'nychteri' and the sweet red 'visanto'. Both of these wines belong to the category 'Appellation of Origin

The old tradition of training the vine stems is typical of the island.

of Superior Quality' (OPAP). The name 'nychteri' derives from the fact that in the past, the procedure of wine-making took place at night, when the temperatures were low and there was no danger that the product would 'turn'. 'Visanto' derives from the Italian 'vin santo' and could mean either 'holy wine' because it was used during Holy Communion, or 'wine of Santorini'. It is made from overripe white grapes which are spread out to dry beneath the burning sun for a number of days, to produce a sweet, concentrated wine with a unique flavour. The wines of Santorini are famed not only in Greece but also abroad, where they have acquired much acclaim and a number of awards.

This recognition fuels the greatest hope of a continuation of the resistance offered by local wine growers to the pressures exerted by the meteoric tourist development of the island.

The traditional way of pruning the vines on Santorini. To protect the plants from the strong winds but also allow them to benefit from the moisture of the soil in the dry island environment, their trunks are wound into low 'coils' which, especially in winter when the leaves have fallen, resemble large birds' nests.

GEOLOGY

The southern Aegean is an area in which the African tectonic plate touches the European plate. The sinking of the African plate led to the creation of an arc of active volcanoes running from Methana via Melos and Santorini to Nisyros, through which a huge mass of magma (molten rock rich in carbonates) is released. Of these volcanoes, the most active is that of Santorini.

A romantic game with volcanic materials.

The first large eruption took place 2.5 million years ago to the south-west of Santorini, near the little Christiana islands. At that time Santorini was a small, non-volcanic island, parts of which are still visible in the non-volcanic limestone of the mountain of Profitis Ilias. Gradually, nearby underwater volcanoes began to produce magma, with the result that numerous small islands were created. Around 500,000 years ago, two huge conical volcanoes had already developed and joined with the original island. Geologists call these Peristeria (the northern cone) and Thera (the southern cone, where the caldera is situated today). Around 300,000 years later, the volcano of Thera began to eject huge quantities of molten rock; the magma chamber emptied completely and the external skin fractured, creating a huge hole - the 'caldera' (the word is Spanish,

Oia, like Fira and Imerovigli, is built on the rim of the caldera.

meaning 'cauldron', or 'cooking pot' and denotes a volcanic hollow with a diameter of more than 1 mile). This procedure was repeated many times over the following 200,000 years; the volcanoes produced magma, broke up, formed again and broke up again in a continuous series of eruptions. The last big eruption, according to the most recent calculations, occurred around 1630 BC and was that which destroyed the prehistoric settlement at Akrotiri; hence it is known as the Minoan eruption. It was the largest eruption to take place during the last 10,000 years of the history of the planet. Comparisons with some other eruptions that have been the subject of closer observation give us an idea of the nature of this terrifying phenomenon.

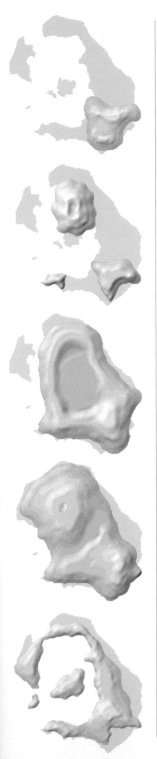

700,000 years ago: the volcano of Akrotiri.

300,000 years ago: the volcano of Peristeri.

200,000 years ago: the caldera "Lower Pumice series".

30,000 years ago: The Skaros volcano.

3,700 years ago: Strongyli.

**New data
which
re-write
History**

A new study using radiocarbon dating (C14) on the trunks and seeds of trees poses the problem of the re-examination of the chronology of the Bronze Age in both the Aegean and the wider area of the eastern Mediterranean. In the journal 'Science' on 28 April 2006, the research group led by Stuart Manning announced the conclusions of their study and placed the eruption of Santorini towards the end of the 17th century BC, and not 100 years later as many have hitherto believed. They went on to say that these findings would perhaps lead to a reconsideration of the history of the Mediterranean civilisations which reached their peak about 3,600 years ago, and of the Bronze Age in general.

Manning and his colleagues analysed 127 measurements of radiocarbon C14 from samples, including sections of tree rings and seeds/fruits from a harvest,

collected on Santorini, Crete, Rhodes and in Turkey. The results, combined with a complex statistical analysis, allowed the researchers to define exact chronologies for the cultural phases towards the end of the Bronze Age, and place the eruption between 1660 and 1613 BC. This chronology conflicts with previous estimations that correlated the Aegean commercial goods found in Egypt and the Near East with Egyptian inscriptions and archives, and dated the eruption to around 1500 BC. Above all, the new results were supported by a dendrochronological study using C14 dating by the Danish palaeobotanist Walter Friedrich, published in the same edition of the journal 'Science'. Friedrich analysed a branch from an olive tree that had been severed during the course of the eruption and dated it to the end of the 17th century BC.

The eruption of 1866 as it was depicted in a magazine of the time.

SANTORIN
ISLAND
ANCIENT THERA

Map dating from 1818. Nea Kammeni has 1/3 of its present size.

had the form of a ring with the modern island joined to Therasia and Aspronisi and an opening between the latter and the place where the lighthouse is situated today. The area inside the ring was covered by sea and in the centre, where the Kammeni islands are located today, there was an island of unknown size on which the volcanic vent was located. During the first phase of the Minoan eruption, relatively small quantities of pumice and tephra were ejected to a height of several kilometres and covered the island in a layer up to six metres thick. In the following, paroxysmal phase a column of pumice and tephra was created which erupted into the atmosphere to a height of around 35km, forming 'mushroom' columns similar

The Santorini volcano produced around 35 times more magma than that of Mount St. Helens in the USA in 1980, and had a degree of explosivity that was ten times greater. The eruption in 1883 of the volcano of Krakatoa in Indonesia, which is smaller than that of Santorini, could be heard over a radius greater than 4,500 km and caused the death of 36,000 people.

Recent discoveries of stromatoliths in the area of Oia have overturned the existing theory that the caldera we see today was created during the Minoan eruption, and have assigned its formation to a previous eruption that took place about 21,000 years earlier. Therefore at the time of the settlement at Akrotiri, Thera

to those caused by atomic bombs, and later falling onto the island. This cloud of tephra, because of the prevailing winds, moved mainly in a south-easterly direction and covered the nearby islands - Crete, Rhodes - and the shores of the whole of the eastern Mediterranean. There may have been global climatic consequences. At the same time, around 30-40 cubic kilometres of magma, incandescent rock and boulders poured out of the crater and covered the whole of the island terrain in a layer of up to 50 metres' thickness. Finally, when the chamber had emptied completely the volcanic structure collapsed, leading to the formation of the central caldera and the straits between Thera and Therasia, as well as between

Therasia and Aspronisi; all of these make up the modern, impressive landscape of Santorini. During the collapse, huge quantities of water rushed in to flood the hollow created, ending this phase of natural activity of really biblical proportions in the most impressive way. The greatest visible height of the walls of the caldera is 385 metres, and the depth of the sea is analogous at the same point.

The mountain called Peristeria has now disappeared, but the mountain of Thera reformed and its peak appeared above the surface of the sea in 197 BC. The first little island to emerge was called Hiera by the people of antiquity; it was followed after the eruption of 46 AD during the reign of the Emperor

Volcanic rocks have become souvenirs, and the volcano itself a sight worth seeing, for thousands of visitors.

| ...áde Kaym | Aphrousse | Nea Kaymene | Volkanos | Baider Molo
Kegel von 1707 | Thrasia | Mikra Kaymene |

Copperplate etching of the eruption of 1866.

Claudius by another island which they called Theia. Due to the tidal wave that this eruption caused, the sea at Levena on Crete receded over the distance of a mile, while volcanic pumice reached the beaches of Asia Minor, Lesvos and Macedonia. This volcanic activity was mentioned by Seneca, Titus Livius, Pliny the Elder, Dio Cassius, Aurelius Victor, Philostratus, Orosius and Cassiodorus. The two little islands were joined together after a third eruption a few years later, in 60 AD. A new eruption increased the size of the island in 726 AD; it was believed to be a sign of Divine wrath against the Byzantine Emperor Leo

III Isaurus, who was an iconoclast. The emperor's opponents used the event to incite insurrection, which finally began in 727, both in the Cyclades as well as in the rest of Greece. References to the volcanic activity during this period were made by Nikiforos, Theophanes and Yiorgios Kedrinos. The increase in the size of the island continued in 1457 and 1508, when the island that is now called Palea Kammeni acquired the shape it has today. In 1573, new volcanic activity gave birth to a little island measuring 500 x 300m, which was called Mikri Kammeni. In 1707 two volcanic cones appeared and joined together five years later to form a third island - Nea Kammeni - between Palea and Mikri Kammeni that was larger and higher than the other two. From 1866 to 1870 there was a phase of strong volcanic activity which led to the tripling in size of Nea Kammeni. From August 1925 to January

Photograph of the volcanic activity of 1850. The emission of gases reduces the likelihood of a new, big eruption.

Nea Kammeni, Palea Kammeni, and Aspronisi in the background.

The Mysterious Island

Strong volcanic activity developed at the beginning of 1866. A first-hand witness of the awakening of the volcano on the morning of 26th January, 1866 was a local warden who happened to be on Nea Kammeni. He observed movements in the ground near to the volcanic cone there. The columns of smoke which were ejected could be seen from Crete. On 10th May, 1866 two little islands appeared out of the sea; these were named the May Islands. They later sank under the waves again and today lie around one metre under the surface. This activity provoked worldwide scientific interest. A large Greek delegation of chemists, geologists, astronomers and engineers arrived on the island; they were joined by a photographer, and this was the first time ever that photography was used for the study of such natural phenomena. The Academie de Paris sent a scientific delegation led by the famous volcanologist F. Fouqué, who was to make a very important contribution to the study of the Santorini volcano. A group of scientists sent by the ruler of Hanover also participated. Amongst the foreigners who came to the island to observe the phenomena was Jules Verne. Much impressed, the author later referred to Santorini in his book "20,000 Leagues under the Sea"; the island was also the inspiration for "The Mysterious Island", in which Captain Nemo and his crew follow the course of a volcanic eruption.

1926 the little islet of Dafni was formed and joined with Mikri and Nea Kammeni into a single island. In 1928, during the period from 1939 to 1941, and finally in 1950, strong volcanic activity led to the formation of volcanic domes.

Palea and Nea Kammeni - called simply the 'volcano' by the local people - constitute the youngest volcanic location in the eastern Mediterranean; the formation of Nea Kammeni began less than 450 years ago, while the last areas of lava were added only about 60 years ago. Today there are seven vents on Nea Kammeni, and one on Palea Kammeni. These all emit gases on a daily basis; the continuous release of pressure reduces the likelihood of a future eruption.

Apart from the volcano located in the middle of the caldera there is also the underwater volcano of Koloumbo to the north east of Santorini, near Oia. The activity of Koloumbo has been recorded; it began with the earthquakes of 1649 and finished in 1650. During this period, which was called "the time of evil" by the local inhabitants, around 70 people and a large number of domestic animals perished, mainly from the poisonous gases which were released in the vicinity over a period of months.

HISTORY

HISTORY

The archaeological finds (sherds of pottery) attest to the human presence on Santorini from the 5th millenium BC onwards, i.e. from the Late Neolithic period. In the Early Bronze Age (Protocycladic period, 3200-2000 BC) a small settlement already existed on the island, while in the subsequent Middle Cycladic period (2000-1700 BC) human activity not only continued but increased to a great degree.

Nippled ewer from Akrotiri, decorated with swallows. End of the 18th century BC. Museum of Prehistoric Thera.

The inhabitants lived in settlements with a high degree of structure and organisation; this is evidenced by the excavations at Akrotiri. This prosperity continued during the first phase of the Late Cycladic period (1700 BC onwards), but around 1630, the eruption of the volcano violently interrupted the progress and destroyed the island. The total area of the ground surface which had not sunk was covered by lava and volcanic dust, making any survival impossible. It seems that the island remained uninhabited until around the end of the 13th century BC at the latest.

The historian Herodotus (Histories, Book IV, 147 ff.) provides us with extensive information about the earlier history of the island, which at that time was called

Female figure in profile. Wall-painting from Akrotiri.

Kalliste because of its beauty, or Strongyli because of its round shape. It was also remembered as Philotera, Tefsia, Kalavria, Therameni and Rineia. The Latin author Justinus referred to it by the name of Therameni, and Porphyrogenitos as Rineia. Also, the form 'Therasia' is met in writings by bishops before the Frankish occupation. During the period of the Turkish occupation it was called Demirzik ('little mill'), perhaps because of the many windmills that existed on the island.

According to mythology, Kadmos, son of Agenor, arrived on the island in his search for Europa who had been kidnapped by Zeus. Either because he was impressed by the beauty of the place or for some other reason, on his departure he left behind some Phoenician comrades, amongst whom was his kinsman Memvliaros. They lived there for eight generations, until Theras arrived on the island. This young man was also a descendant of Kadmos and had lived in Sparta as a guardian and regent for his nephews who had not yet come of age. He had left his homeland with the agreement of the Lacedaemonians in order to save some fugitive Minyae whom he brought in three triaconters to Santorini, where his distant relatives lived. There, on the summit of the mountain they built a fortified city which was named Thera after its founder. This name extended to stand for the whole island, which from then on and during the whole of the historic period was considered a Dorian area. Around the beginning of the 9th century BC Thera, like Crete and Melos, adopted the Phoenician alphabet to meet the requirements of the Greek language. Caught in the wake of conservative Sparta and because of the tribal descent of its inhabitants, Thera did not follow the cultural progress of the other Aegean islands and was subjected to only a few influences from its neighbours. During the Archaic period (7th and 6th centuries BC) it had some contacts at first with Crete and then later with Rhodes, Corinth and also Athens and Ionia. However, such contacts were superficial and did not exert any influence on the closed society of the island. It is indicative of this fact that exactly during this period of great colonising activities by the Greek city-states, the inhabitants of Thera only founded one colony, that of Cyrene on

Archaic statue of a girl dating from the 7th century BC. Archaeological Museum of Thera.

"...They arrived on the island, picked up the man whom they had left behind there and then built a city on the shore of Libya, on the coast opposite the island in a place called Aziris where there are two beautiful meadows crossed by a river."
(Herodotus Histories Book IV, 150-157).

From the Phoenician to the Greek alphabet

"Those Phoenicians who had come with Kadmos...taught the Greeks a number of things, and in particular writing, of which, I believe, they had hitherto been ignorant. In the beginning their letters were those that were used by all Phoenicians, but as time passed their pronounciation changed and with it the shape of the letters. In most regions the neighbours of the Phoenicians were Ionian Greeks. They were taught writing by the Phoenicians, and after modifying the letters a little, began to use them but still called them Phoenician letters, which was quite correct since the Phoenicians had brought them to Greece." (Herodotus Histories V, 58) Modern epigraphical research has corroborated the information given to us by the 5th century Greek historian. Proof of where and how the idea for a Greek alphabet originated lies in the shape of the symbols itself, their order of succession and their names (which at the same time provide acrophonic values for the sounds), as well as the fact that Greek was first written from right to left, like Phoenician. However, at this point Greek genius intervened; as it has done in other spheres it developed and perfected with unique dynamic energy what it had received from other civilisations. The Phoenicians seemed content with a script that expressed only consonants; filling in the vowels was left to recognition of the words and to syntactic context. The Greeks developed the Phoenician script with the addition of special symbols for the vowels and thus led it towards perfection. In order to achieve this, they chose the four Phoenician symbols for consonants which did not have any particular application where the value of sounds was concerned, i.e Aleph, He, Jod, and Ajin or Ojin, for the expression of the vowels a,e,i,o, and for u they chose the vowel-related Vav.

As to the place where the Greeks first acquired the Phoenician alphabet, glossological studies and very old inscriptions found still in situ point to either Rhodes or Thera. In fact, on the site of the ancient city of Thera there are numerous inscriptions hewn into stones or the rock, rather like early graffiti. Most of them are grouped around the sanctuary of Apollo Karneios at the south-eastern tip of Ancient Thera, where rites involving naked children were celebrated, and around the Gymnasium. Many of the graffiti are of a religious or erotic nature, the latter kind sometimes particularly explicit. These inscriptions are of tremendous importance. Apart from constituting a body of evidence for the study of the spiritual and material life of a Doric city during the Geometric and Early Archaic periods, they are the oldest Greek inscriptions, dating from before the 8th century BC, and give us a glimpse of the first form of the alphabet and the dialect of the period. Many are written in the 'boustrophedon' manner, i.e. 'as an ox ploughs' from right to left and then left to right.

Aleph
Beth
Gimel
Daleth
He
Vav
Zajin
Cheth
Teth
Jod
Kaph
Lamed
Mem
Nun
Samech
Ajin
Pe
Ssade
Qoph
Resch
Schin
Tav

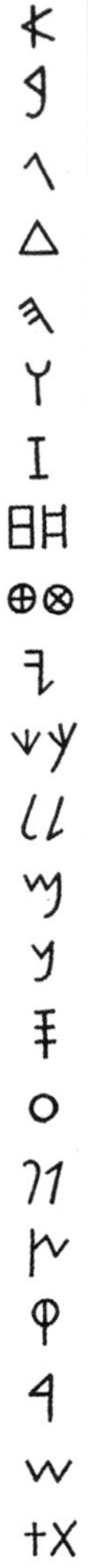

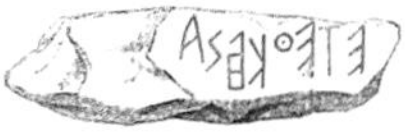

Above: fragment of an inscription from Sellada. Left: inscription on a rock in Ancient Thera. From the book 'Thera' by Hiller von Gaertringen.

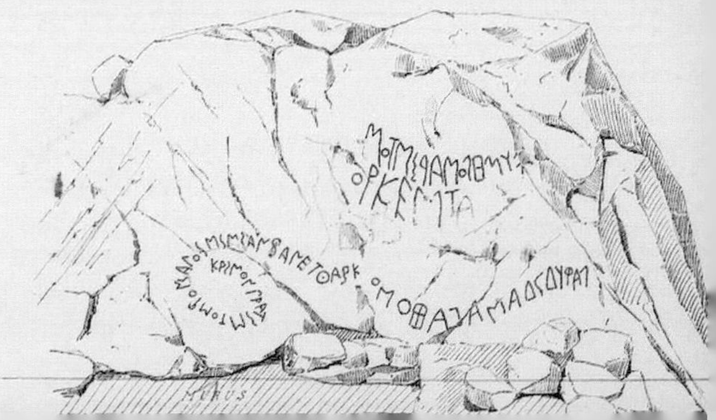

Relief of a dolphin from Ancient Thera.

Silver stater from Thera, 550-500 BC.

the shore of North Africa. As Herodotus informs us, this was not the result of any wish on their part, but of necessity.

In the 6th century BC Thera minted its own coinage bearing a representation of two dolphins, the official emblem of the island. At the beginning of the 5th century BC the mint was closed, and resumed its activity after the end of the Athenian hegemony, i.e. around the middle of the 4th century BC. During the military campaign of Xerxes against Greece, Thera was one of the islands which offered land and water to the Persians. After the end of the Median Wars, only Thera, Melos, Anafi and Folegandros did not become members of the Athenian Alliance in 476 BC, because of their predominantly Doric element. Later on, however, Thera was obliged to submit to the thalassocracy of the Athenians and had to pay a levy of three talents

at the beginning of the Peloponnesian War in 425 BC. Nevertheless, during the whole of the Classical period (5th and 4th centuries BC), the conservatism and inclination towards isolation of its inhabitants resulted in Thera not playing a role in the political and cultural forming of Greece. During the period of the wars between the successors of Alexander the Great, the Ptolemies used the island as a base for their war campaigns.

Thera also enjoyed no particular significance during the Roman and Byzantine periods, when it came under the so-called Eparchia of the Islands - island number twenty-nine in the catalogue of Hierokles. The capital of the Eparchia was Rhodes, whose bishopric also held religious jurisdiction over the island. Funerary inscriptions and other religious symbols found on Thera indicate that Christianity arrived on the island at an early date. In 342

The oldest coins produced in the Greek area come from the Aegean islands and date from the beginning of the 6th century BC. It is generally accepted that the first people to mint coins were the Aeginetans. The trend set by Aegina was soon followed by other islands, where the Aeginetan prototypes were used as models. Thus for example, the coinage of Andros had an amphora on the obverse, that of Serifos a frog, that of Tenos a bunch of grapes, that of Naxos a wine cup, and that of Delos a lyre. The coins produced by Thera around 500 BC are also of this type; the emblem chosen for the obverse of the silver stater of Thera comprised two dolphins swimming in opposite directions. This elegant picture exudes a harmonious sense of movement which recalls that of the coinage of Karpathos, produced around the same time.

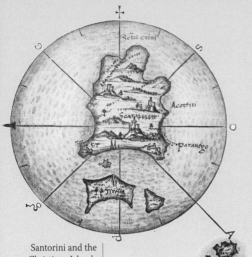

Santorini and the Christiana Islands from the Isolario of Bartolomeo da li Sonetti, Venice 1485.

Map of Santorini according to Gaspare Tentivo, 1683.

the diocese of Thera was founded; its first bishop was Dioskouros. The bishopric was abolished in 1207. The island owes its modern name of Santorini (Santa Irini) to a church dedicated to Saint Irini, which either stood in Perissa or in Riva on Therasia. It is generally believed that the name dates from the period of the Frankish occupation of the island (1207-1537), but it was already called Santorini in 1153 by the Arab geographer Edrizi. The old name of Thera, corrupted into Fira, has survived as the name given to the main town on the island.

Given the fact that the island was of little significance during the Byzantine period, it is rather strange that the Emperor Alexios Komnenus (1081-1118) built the church of Panayia Episkopi there.

In 1207, following the sack of Constantinople by the Crusaders of the 4th Crusade in 1204, Thera was occupied

by Marco Sanoudo, who then gave it to Jacovo Barozzi. In 12 it was liberated by the Byzanti who expelled the Frankish occupiers, but during the seve years' war between Androniko Palaeologos and Venice, Baroz annexed Thera and Therasia. In 1335 Nikolaos I Sanoudos of Naxos attacked the Barozzis and drove them from their baronetcy, adding the two islan to the Duchy of Naxos where they remained for a period of 8 years. Then Duke Ioannis Iaco Crispo gave Thera to his brot Nikolao Crispo, despot of Syr and Therasia to his other broth Marco Crispo, despot of Ios. B the middle of the 15th century once rich island had suffered su great damage from constant pi attacks that it supported only 300 inhabitants and yielded an annual tax of only 500 ducats. I 1480, Thera was given as a dow to Domenico Pizani, son of the Duke of Crete and member of a great Venetian family. During h time, the island managed to hea its wounds and acquire a little prosperity. However, in 1492 Venice once again handed Ther to the Duchy of Naxos. During the period of Frankish occupati many of its inhabitants embrac Catholicism.

In 1537 the Turkish storm also raged over Thera, and the islan was conquered by Haireddin Barbarossa. He wrested Kea, Mykonos and Santorini from th Latins, forcing them to recognis the supremacy of the Supreme Pforte. In 1579 after the death of the Spanish Jew Joseph Nazi, to whom the Cyclades had been given by the Sultan, Santorini

Map of Santorini
by the Dutch
cartographer Olfert
Dapper, 1688.

became a direct Turkish possession but enjoyed such privileges as to be almost autonomous. The inhabitants turned their efforts to trading and shipping and had close contacts with the great centres of the period such as Constantinople, Odessa and Alexandria, founding considerable colonies there. In 1770 the population of the island reached 9,000 and judging from the amount of tax which these inhabitants paid, they must have been more prosperous than the inhabitants of the other islands. This great affluence led, at the beginning of the 19th century, to Thera owning the third largest merchant fleet in Greece after Hydra and Spetses. The mansions - mostly captains'

Emborio, in a
coloured etching
on a drawing by
J.P.Hilaire, 1782.

Boats in the caldera. Drawing by M.G.F.A. Choiseul-Gouffier.

The 'Proton', built in 1898, was one of the first Greek steamships. Nautical Museum, Oia.

residences - which are still preserved in the villages on the island bear witness to this economic flowering. On 5th May, 1821, the day of the celebration of Ayia Irini, patron saint of the island, Evangelos Mavzarakis who had been installed on the island as a representative of Dimitris Ypsilanti, raised the flag of freedom and drove out the Turkish authorities.

In 1856 Thera had 269 ships, which brought wealth to the islanders. This is illustrated by a testimony of the time: "Gold and silver flowed in, the [ships] brought in dollars and baskets full to the brim, the captains' houses were rich and there was good fortune in the houses of the boatswains and sailors. Festivities lasted from one night to the next."

ΠΡΣ

However, the appearance of steamships in the 20th century and the inability of the inhabitants to keep pace with developments marked the decline of Santorini, as of other cities in Greece concerned with shipping. Still, until the 2nd World War, 75% of the island population were engaged in shipping. The final blow was dealt in 1956 by the great earthquake; the destruction forced part of the population to abandon the island. There followed a period of economic attrition until the decade of the 1970s, when the island was 're-discovered' by modern travellers. Since then, tourism has constituted the main occupation of

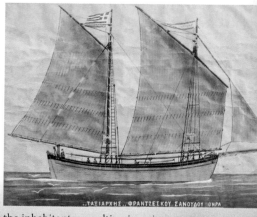

..ΤΑΞΙΑΡΧΗΣ.. ΦΡΑΝΤΖΕΙΚΟΥ ΣΑΝΟΥΔΟΥ ΘΗΡΑ

the inhabitants, resulting in economic progress but at the same time the abandonment of traditional agricultural activities, with the exception of vine-growing which has enjoyed a great flowering in recent years.

The arrival of steamships heralded the end of the 'Taxiarchi' (above) and also of the other Theran sailing ships. Nautical Museum, Oia.

THE EXCAVATIONS

The first archaeological excavations on the island took place after the liberation of Greece in the mid-19th century. In 1856, inscriptions dating from the Roman period were discovered at Kamari; this led to its identification with Ancient Thera.

A little later on, the quarrying of Theran earth and the removal of huge quantities of surface material brought to light the first traces of prehistoric building remains; the first excavation was begun by the Greek physician D. Nomikos in 1866 and continued by the French geologist F. Fouqué. Three years later, members of the French School of Archaeology examined prehistoric remains in the wider area of Akrotiri, not far from the place where the large archaeological site is located today. During the last five years of the 19th century Hiller von Gärtringen conducted a large-scale excavation at Mesa Vouno which revealed the remains of the ancient city of Thera. The research carried out during the first half of the 20th century was limited and did not yield impressive results until 1960, when the Greek Archaeological Society under N. Zafeiropoulos excavated the extensive cemetery of Sellada.

In 1967 the excavation at Akrotiri was begun by Spyridon Marinatos. All the signs were propitious where the choice of the site for excavation was concerned. Apart from the existence of sherds of pottery on the surface, the terrain was extremely level and thus would have been suitable for prehistoric settlement; it was also near the sea and on the part of the shore nearest to Crete. What actually led Marinatos to make his final decision was the fact that the ground was known to give way frequently under the weight of the pack animals which passed through the area. The excavation continued until the death of Marinatos in 1974 on the very site that he had discovered; thereafter, it was resumed by C. Doumas.

Spyridon Marinatos at the Akrotiri excavations, in a photograph by the great Greek photographer Spyros Meletzis

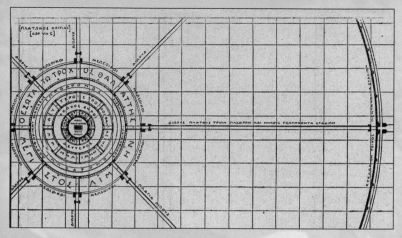

The myth of Atlantis

"Indeed, at that time you could cross that sea because at its entrance, which you call the Pillars of Herakles, there was an island which was larger than Libya and Asia put together. And you could pass to the other islands from it, and to the continent opposite which surrounded the true ocean.... Well, on this island, Atlantis, things were well ordered..... After quite a time had passed, however, there was a great earthquake followed by floods, and in one terrible day and night the earth swallowed up all your army, while Atlantis sank beneath the waves..." Plato, Timaios 24e-25d.

"First of all, we must remember that a total of nine thousand years had passed since the war that was fought between those who lived outside the Pillars of Herakles and all those who inhabited the lands inside. I should therefore mention the war in detail. It is said that the rule over all who lived inside was enjoyed by this city until the end of the war, while the leaders of the others [those outside] were the kings of the island of Atlantis, which, as we said before, was larger than Libya and Asia put together. Now that it has sunk because of the earthquakes, it has been covered by mud, forming a barrier which hinders those who want to pass to the ocean that lies beyond..." Plato, Kritias, 109e - 109a.

It is these fragments of the Platonic dialogues which have sparked off a continuing series of discussions about the lost continent of Atlantis; the philological arguments abound and even if they

The metropolis of Atlantis according to Plato's description. Drawing by Patroklos Kabanakis.

Plato

35

are not always substantiated, the subject retains its attraction. Plato's sources were already doubted from antiquity onwards, as well as the existence of the city that the philosopher had had in his mind.

In both dialogues, Kritias tells Socrates, Timaios and Hermokrates what he, as a ten-year-old, heard from his ninety-year-old grandfather of the same name. During his discourse he alludes to the teachings which Solon brought back from the Egyptian priests at Saïs. Solon believed that the priests were wiser than himself and indeed wiser than all the men he had ever met, and in order to make them tell him more, he related what the Greeks knew about the time of Deucalion's flood. He was surprised, however, to hear that before the latter flood there were three other global calamities, and that outside the Pillars of Herakles there had once existed Atlantis, an island larger than Asia and Libya (i.e. Africa) put together. Via Atlantis and other nearby islands, it was possible to pass from the old world to the continent that was located beyond. An important civilisation had developed in Atlantis. The land was ruled by the descendants of Atlantos, son of Poseidon. At some point they amassed their forces and tried to conquer Greece and Egypt, but the Athenians, leading the defenders, showed particular heroism and preserved their freedom and that of the other peoples. However, after quite a period of time had passed, there was a terrible cataclysm which destroyed the whole world, and Atlantis disappeared beneath the sea. This happened 9,000 years before the time of Solon. After Plato, other

Greek writers concerned themselves with Atlantis. Aristotle considered the whole account to be a fabrication by Plato, while others found a historical basis in it. In more recent times the lost continent has continued to delight people's fantasy and has thus featured more in poetry than in science. Francis Bacon praised the advance of science in the 'New Atlantis', Frascator (16th century) wrote a great poem in Latin which was translated into French by Dr. Yvaren (1847), and Nepomucene Lemercier produced the epic 'Atlantis'. The most famous eulogist of Atlantis was the Catalan poet Jacinto Verdaguer, whose epic poem was translated into many languages and constituted a source of inspiration for many artists.

The basic questions posed by Plato's account are:

a) Did Atlantis really exist?
b) Where was it located?
c) How was it destroyed
d) When did this destruction take place?

A lot of ink has been wasted on this questions for centuries but not one of them has been completely and convincingly answered. Especially where the location of the mythical continent is concerned, various parts of the planet have been suggested, such as America, Palestine, the Scandinavian Peninsula, the North Pole, Europe, the area around Gibraltar, and also further to the south, the western edge of the Sahara. K. Frost was the first to connect the myth with Minoan Crete in 1909. He believed that the story was created by the Egyptians when, after the conquest of Crete by the Mycenaeans, connections between the island and Egypt were suddenly interrupted. A. Galanopoulos also identified Atlantis with Santorini, basing his arguments on geological studies. A similar theory was supported by Spyridon Marinatos; his basic thesis was that the eruption of the volcano, which in his opinion had taken place around 1450 BC, coincided with the destruction of Minoan Crete and the attack on Egypt by the 'Sea Peoples' - amongst whom were the Tursi, Sekeli and Sardana (probably the Tyrrhenians, Sicilians and Sardinians). Since they would have come from the western Mediterranean, they may perhaps have given the impression of having an Atlantic origin. Where the chronology of the catastrophe is concerned, Marinatos believed that if the figure of 9,000 years which has come down to us is corrected to 900, we have the correct length of the space of time between the catastrophe in 1550 BC and the 600 BC date for Solon, when the story was recounted.

It is apparent that the very ancient myth still retains its secret. We should perhaps ask if the great fascination that it continues to evoke on a global scale is due to the strangeness and charm of the story, or to some remnants of our collective memory.

A picture of the settlement. The volcanic tephra covering it have left it almost intact.

AKROTIRI

The prehistoric settlement at Akrotiri is one of the most important archaeological sites in the Aegean, and research there has contributed decisively to the understanding of the civilisation of the region from the 4th to mid 2nd century BC.

The ancient name of the settlement is unknown to us and for this reason the name of the modern village has been given to it. It lies in the south of the island on a little plain, and had two harbours which were sheltered from the north winds that blow constantly in the Aegean. One of the harbours still exists; the other has silted up over the course of time. The morphology of the terrain likewise favoured the development of agricultural activities. Finds of pottery attest that the area was already inhabited in the Late Neolithic period; this first settlement must have been limited to the area where Xeste 3 was later built. The existence of a settlement is also certain during the Protocycladic period, even though only very sparse remains of buildings have been preserved. During the following period - the Middle Cycladic - the town, built in what was a strategic location on the island, was transformed into an important cosmopolitan port. It had close relations and carried on cultural and commercial exchange

In fine weather, the mountain massif of Psiloritis and the White Mountains can be seen on the horizon. The proximity of Crete to the settlement at Akrotiri played a decisive role in its prosperity throughout its history.

It was on the ruins left by one such earthquake that the last settlement - that of the Late Cycladic IA period which was destroyed definitively by the eruption of the volcano around 1630 BC - was built. The eruption was also preceded by a strong earthquake which drove the inhabitants from the settlement and forced them into temporary shelters. They returned during the period between the earthquake and the eruption to secure their belongings and to repair their houses. The complete absence from the city of both human skeletal remains as well as jewellery and transportable precious objects in general, is evidence that the volcano 'warned' the inhabitants and gave them time to abandon their hearths for good, taking their valuables with them.

It is believed that the final catastrophe took place in spring, because grains of pollen from olive and pine trees were found in the layer of eruptive material. The settlement was covered by a thick layer of volcanic tephra to a depth of 15 metres, which has contributed to its excellent state of preservation. Its careful excavation and the world-renowned work of the conservators have combined to yield artefacts which enable us to reconstruct the activities and daily life of the inhabitants.

with Crete, the rest of the Cyclades, mainland Greece, the Dodecanese, Syria, Palestine, and Egypt; its vessels traversed the eastern Mediterranean, taking basic commodities and luxury goods to various destinations. Meanwhile, the original town was extended and developed into an urban centre with a notable building density, network of streets, and drainage system. Due to its extension, the inhabitants had to abandon use of the ancient burial site and transfer the cemetery to another location; the latter has not yet been discovered. Most of the buildings which survived until the final destruction were constructed in this period, but they exhibit numerous repairs made necessary because of the frequent earthquakes.

The architecture, wall-paintings, pottery, stone or metal, tools, and the wooden furniture all combine to make a complete world which holds the same fascination for the everyday visitor as it does for the experienced researcher.

The square to the north of Xeste 3.

Plaster cast of a bed from room Δ2. Here, even the details of the rope that bound the leather to the wooden frame are visible. Thanks to the careful work of the excavators who poured plaster into the hollow space, we have an exact moulded cast, and thus it has been possible to produce a replica in wood and leather of a piece of furniture that was made 3,500 years ago. The plaster cast is on display in the National Archaeological Museum, Athens.

The architecture

The final prehistoric settlement had all the characteristics of a well-organised city: a network of roadways with paved streets, squares, an underground drainage system, administrative and religious buildings, and houses with sanitary installations. In general terms, the settlement has much in common with the modern villages of the Cyclades. The little alleyways are winding and narrow, with a width that is not constant and is sometimes reduced by the façade of a house, or sometimes increased to form a little, irregularly-shaped 'square'. The houses are cube-like, the roofs flat and the materials used for the building are those which the landscape of the island offered the inhabitants: stone, clay, bricks strengthened with straw, gypsum, and a little wood.

The houses were two- or three-storeyed. The walls were constructed with bricks of clay into which straw had often been mixed in order to give greater strength and durability. Often, the corners of the house were constructed from large ashlar blocks, giving the building greater stability. In some houses of individuals who were wealthy or of particular importance we find whole facades with a revetement of ashlar blocks, and for this reason the archaeologists have called them 'xestes'. This type of construction had a strengthening framework of large stone joists which also afforded it elasticity during the frequent earthquakes. The floors on the ground level were generally of compacted earth, but floors paved with stone slabs are not infrequently found. The entrances to the houses were usually paved with stone. The floors of the upper storeys were constructed with wooden joists covered by a layer of reeds or branches. A layer of earth was added on top of the latter, and this was sometimes covered with stone slabs, the joints between them occasionally painted in colours; the latter was of a particularly luxurious standard and not often found. In other instances, the floor consisted of frag-

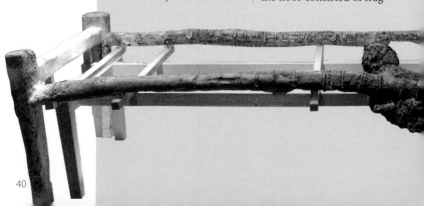

ments of seashells or pebbles, although these were not arranged pictorially in any way. The houses had many openings, either doors or large windows, which were surrounded by wooden beams or hewn blocks. Both the interior and exterior walls of the buildings were covered in plaster. For the external surfaces and those in storage areas the plaster was made from a mixture of clay and straw, while a fine-grained limestone plaster was used in the rooms; in those on ground level it was usually monochrome, while in the rooms on the upper floors it was decorated with wall-paintings. Until very recently, no house had been found without at least one room containing wall-paintings. However, the newest researches in the north of the settlement have brought to light houses that are of a more modest type and do not have the luxurious decoration of those in the central neighbourhood; it is, however, perhaps too early to draw any conclusions from these discoveries.

The roofs of the houses were flat and built with the same technique that was applied to the floors of the upper storeys; compacted earth served as an insulating material which ensured warmth in the winter and coolness in the summer.

The spaces and rooms in the large and well-built houses of the settlement were put to a variety of uses.

On the ground floor there were often storage rooms where the inhabitants kept large pithoi containing foodstuffs such as barley, pulses, olive oil, wine etc. The little cylindrical millstones that were found in nearly all the houses indicate that the grinding of some grains or pulses took place on the spot. Little windows secured the ventilation of the rooms and the good conservation of what was stored there. Larger windows that can be discerned in some ground floor spaces indicate that they were used as shops or workshops. The living quarters were on the upper floors. All of the buildings had sanitary installations on the ground floor or upper floors, as is clear from the cylindrical clay pipes which were built into the walls and carried waste directly away to the central drainage conduit.

Equipment for the milling of grain.

Nothing remains of the individual pieces of furniture in the houses. The organic, decayed materials from which they were made did not survive the volcanic destruction and the course of time, but in exceptional circumstances they left their imprints in the tephra layer. To date, 4 beds, 4 stools, and 3 three-legged tables have been reconstructed. Likewise, valuable information has been preserved regarding basketry, rope-making, wooden box and barrel-making, and also the preparation of leather.

Broken three-legged cauldrons from the excavation at Akrotiri.

A VISIT TO THE ARCHAEOLOGICAL SITE

Of a total area of 20,000 sq metres that has been suggested by archaeologists as the total size of the settlement, only 10,000 sq metres have been uncovered. Of the buildings that have already been located, a number have not been fully examined, thus many surprises are still to be expected. Also - probably for practical reasons - some parts of the excavation are not accessible to the public. Nevertheless, the degree of preservation of the buildings and their great antiquity make Akrotiri one of the most important and most attractive archaeological sites in the Mediterranean.

Xeste 3

TThe first building that the visitor comes upon, in the western part of the site, is Xeste 3. This is large, carefully-designed, and constructed with ashlar blocks. The building was at least two-storeyed, as can be deduced from the staircase in the shape of the Greek letter Π which began from the space immediately behind the entrance (5). Each floor had 14 rooms, most of which were decorated with wall-paintings. In Vestibule 5 two

XESTE 5

CENOTAPH (EMPTY TOMB)

SECTOR A

BUILDING H

XESTE 1

MILL

STREET OF THE CURETES

BUILDING Θ

HOUSE OF THE LADIES

SQUARE OF THE CENOTAPH

The archaeological site of Akrotiri.

BUILDING Z

SQUARE OF THE CONVOY

WEST HO

Rooms with wall-paintings.

- - Visitors' entrance

human figures were depicted; they have been designated as 'huntsmen'.

The frieze of the monkeys and the crocus flowers, the wall-painting with the rosettes and the rhomboid designs, and that of the Naked Boys also come from this building. Room 3B on the first floor was decorated with a procession of women of whom one is carrying a small basket and another has bunches of wild roses. In room 3A on the first floor there was the famous representation of the female Saffron Gatherers and that of the Mistress of the Animals, which constituted part of the same thematic composition.

In the corresponding room on the ground floor there was a Lustral Basin - a sacred place that is well known from the Minoan palaces. On the north wall of the same room a wall-painting depicted female Adorants. The existence of a Lustral Basin, together with the subject-matter of the paintings and the monumental façade of the

Detail of the ducks and dragonflies from the necklece of the Mistress of the Animals.

XESTE 4

BUILDING IA

BUILDING I

STREET OF THE CURETES

XESTE 2

E

BUILDING IB

SQUARE OF THE MONKEYS

BUILDING B

Δ

MILL SQUARE

SQUARE OF XESTE 3

GLE
RE

TELCHINES STREET

BUILDING Π

HOUSE OF THE ANCHOR

BUILDING Γ

SQUARE OF THE LUSTRAL BASIN

XESTE 3

HOUSE OF THE BENCHES

BUILDING ΣΤ

The Telchines

The Telchines were a mythical race from Rhodes whose nine founders originated from Crete and went first to Cyprus before arriving on Rhodes, which as Strabo (14, 653) tells us was once called Telchinis "after the Telchines who made the island their home". Crete is also referred to as Telchinia. The Telchines were considered to be sons of the Sea, the Sky and the Land and were described as creatures without legs, but with wings instead of arms. It was believed that they taught Man the arts and crafts, and gave him other useful knowledge and inspiration to work with metals.

building, led the excavators to conclude that Xeste 3 was a public shrine.

House of the Benches

The discovery of one of the few valuable objects from the excavations, the unique gold statuette of an ibex, was made during work undertaken to support the roof over the site in the vicinity of this building. The statuette had been kept in a wooden case, of which the imprint has been preserved, and it was found inside a clay larnax beneath a large number of horns, mainly those of goats and sheep.

Square at Xeste 3

This is the name given by the excavators to the space east of the building of the same name.

Telchines Street

A little further to the east there begins the so-called Telchines Street, which is the largest street excavated at the site to date and probably led to the harbour. Although it

has a generally north-south alignment, it deviates in some places to form right angles which recall the little passageways of the modern settlements on the island. Its width varies, while at some points it widens to such an extent that it forms little squares, such as the 'Mill Square' or the 'Triangle Square'.

Building Γ (Gamma)

On the left-hand, western side of the road there is Building Γ which was destroyed to a considerable degree; it has not been thoroughly investigated. In rooms 1 and 2 stone columns had been erected to repair the damage suffered by the building from the earthquake that preceded the great volcanic eruption.

Building B (Beta)

This building, which had at least one upper storey, lies on the right-hand, eastern side of the street. On the south wall of room B1 there was the wall-painting of the Boxing

Telchines Street and Triangle Square.

Boys, and on the west wall the superb painting of the Antelopes. These animals were also depicted both on the east wall (2) and on the north wall (one on each side of the window there). The north and west walls of room B6 were decorated with the wall-painting of the Blue Monkeys.

In the magazine on the ground floor of the building, there were two rows of large vessels set into the wall of a kind of staircase. Since these vessels were immovable, smaller vessels such as the conical rhyta which were found at the same location would have been used to empty them of their contents.

Mill Square

The Mill Square opens out where the two buildings end.

The square takes its name from the equipment for the milling of grain that was found in room B15 of Building Δ opposite.

Building Δ (Delta)

In actual fact, this complex comprises four buildings. The northern section of it is known as Xeste 1. On the ground floor the complex consisted of more than 20 rooms, and at least three staircases led to one or two more storeys. One of the rooms (Δ1) was especially spacious and divided down the middle by a pier-and-door partition ('polythyro'), i.e. openings in a wall one next to the other. This feature is known to us from the Cretan palaces. When opened,

Plaster cast of a carved wooden table from Akrotiri.

The wall-painting with the Blue Monkeys.

the doors folded back into adjacent hollows, giving the impression that the walls had disappeared and been replaced by a row of pilasters. In room Δ2, three walls were covered by a wall-painting with a wonderful composition, that of a rocky landscape with lilies and swallows, the so-called 'Spring Fresco'. The fourth, eastern wall contained a door and a double window. In the north wall there was a little doorway which led to another room. Above the wall-paintings was a narrow blue band which defined the place at which a shelf had been fixed. The surface above this band was painted red. A Mycenaean pithos found in the same room contained nineteen Mycenean 'askoi', the vessels stacked and apparently ready for transport. There was also a hollow cast left by a wooden bed. The fact that cult objects were found outside the room leads to the conclusion that it was a place which had ritual significance. Room Δ16 was most probably a potter's workshop; in room 18A fragments of an inscription in Linear A script were found, and in room 18B a large number of clay seals, probably of Cretan origin. The building had five entrances, of which the western one was accentuated through a propylon. The latter, which projected out into the roadspace, had openings in it in the manner of a stoa. Towards the north, the building formed another open space, known as 'Triangle Square'.

Detail with swallows and lilies from the Spring Fresco.

Sherds bearing signs in the Linear A script. Museum of Prehistoric Thera.

West House

On the north side of this square there is the West House. Next to the entrance to the house there was a large window and behind it the staircase that led to the upper floor. On the ground floor there were magazines, workshops, a kitchen and a place where grain was milled. Room Δ5 on the first floor must have been the most important in the house. There were openings in two of the walls of this room, thus the artist who decorated it made

The fresco depicting the sea battle.

use of the narrow surfaces of the pilasters (representation of the Flower Vase with lilies, and the wall-painting of the 'Young Priestess') or the spaces near the corners (two representations of Fishermen). Beneath the windows there was a band painted to resemble marbling, while above them there was a frieze with the Miniature frescoes. One is known as the 'Fresco of the Flotilla', another depicts a sea battle. The frieze of the River Landscape originates from the same room, and the representations of 'Ikria' from

the adjacent room Δ4. A thin wall separated the latter from room 4A, which was a privy.

'Andiro' (raised area) of the beds

To the north west of the Mill Square there was an open space in which the imprints of three small wooden beds with rope netting were found. Plaster casts were made from them.

House of the Anchor

To the north of the Mill Square there is a house which takes its name from a black stone with a hole through it,

The fresco depicting a river. A number of wild animals and plants can be observed.

The wooden bed from the room with the Spring fresco.

The settlement was abandoned suddenly before the eruption and covered immediately afterwards with volcanic tephra. This resulted in the discovery of a place which gives the impression that it was 'alive' and still inhabited only a few hours ago. Everyday objects were found in locations where they had 'just' been used by their owners; there were also rarer finds, such as a basket in which the spines of the sea urchins it once contained are still preserved. Athens, National Archaeological Museum.

weighing 65 kg, which was probably used as an anchor.

Square of the Empty tomb (Cenotaph)

The area to the north of Sector Δ (Delta) must have been transformed into a square during Late Helladic I, the final phase of the history of the city. A trapezoidal structure was found there which resembles a tomb; it contained 17 Early Cycladic marble figurines and fragments of marble vessels, but no bones - hence the name given to this square today (Square of the Cenotaph or empty tomb). Possibly, this find constitutes an instance of the removal of relics from an earlier cemetery because of the enlargement of the city.

House of the Ladies

Beyond the West House,

Telchines Street has been destroyed by a more recent torrent. A little further to the north the House of the Ladies has been preserved; this owes its name to the wall-paintings which depict two women, found in room 1. The wall-painting with the representation of sea daffodils (previously identified as papyrus) comes from the same room. There was a light-well in the middle of the house.

Sector A

Further north lies the area where excavations began in 1967. This is Sector A or the Magazine of the Pithoi, where a large number of huge storage jars were found still in situ. Some bore linear decoration, spirals or other geometric patterns, others had relief decoration, often of rings or simple wavy lines. All of the pithoi have handles or little holes to enable them to be moved with the help of ropes. The lids of many have been preserved.
In this area, pieces of the wall-paintings of the African, the Adorant monkeys and the Blue Bird were found.

The Mill

AImmediately next to the magazine there was a mill installation. Here, excavation brought to light a very moving

Pithos with dolphins and water fowl. Museum of Prehistoric Thera.

In the most recent excavations a large quantity of organic materials such as rope, leather, cloth remains, baskets, wooden handles of tools, the remains of rush mats, woven plant fibres attached to the handles of bronze utensils etc. came to light. Among the more noteworthy finds are the three wooden 'rattles', 9cm in length, which have been preserved due to the painstaking work of conservators. Two of the three form a pair; they are shaped like human hands with closed fingers and terminate at the wrist in a ring. The underside of each rattle is level and smooth, while on the upper surface the anatomical details are rendered in relief. Rattles of this kind are known to us from Minoan seals and also from Egypt where, made of the bones or teeth of animals or of wood, they were used as musical instruments.

find - that of a basket that contained fish and sea urchins. Two further building complexes, Xeste 2 and Xeste 4 which lie on the eastern side of the settlement, have not yet been exhaustively studied. The northern façade of Xeste 2 is preserved up to the third floor level.

Xeste 4 is the largest of the complexes which have been discovered to date and was probably a public building. In room 2 parts of a frieze were found depicting a boar's tusk helmet of the so-called Mycenaean type, and the fill of room 14 yielded three wooden 'rattles' in the shape of a hand. The street which passed to the south of Xeste 4 has been named the Street of the Curetes.

Wall-painting from the House of the Ladies.

THE WALL-PAINTINGS

Detail from the wall-painting of the Saffron-Gatherers.

Among the most important finds from the excavations, and certainly the most interesting from an aesthetic point of view, are the wall-paintings which decorated most of the buildings in the settlement. Although they are usually designated as frescoes, the technique of their construction is not exactly that of fresco, even though it seems that some preparation such as smoothing of the surface and the marking of the field to be decorated with a thin string took place when the surface was still fresh. The surface may still have been fresh and wet when painting began, but the artists could have continued their work when it had already dried. The smoothing aimed at the creation of a surface which would make it easy for the artist to render the details of his composition, and was carried out with the use of pebbles which had been carefully collected from the beaches of the island - hundreds of such pebbles were found on the site. The colours used were indelible, of mineral or metal oxide origin, simple and pure:

white (from limestone), red (from oxide of iron), black (from charcoal), yellow (from ochre), blue (from silicon with copper and calcium oxides). It is surprising that the purple colour in the details of the fresco of the Saffron Gatherers is that acquired from murex; this indicates a high level of technical knowledge. The subject-matter of the wall-paintings is very varied. An unsurpassed elegance and liveliness unfolds before our eyes in scenes from the everyday life and occupations of the inhabitants, festivals, landscapes, religious rites, and there are also animals in great variety. Antelopes, deer, bulls, goats, sheep, lions and other felines, monkeys, ducks, swallows, fish and dolphins, even butterflies and dragonflies indicate to us the interest which the animal kingdom aroused in prehistoric Man.

At first sight, the similarity with the frescoes of Minoan Crete is clear. The human forms are always rendered with the face in profile but the eyes to the front. The upper part of the body is usually shown *en face* and when presented in profile, the result is usually clumsy. The legs are always rendered in profile. The convention is retained of depicting the men with red, the women with white, and animals are frequently blue. This observation certainly

reinforces the opinion that the well-known fresco of the Saffron-gatherer from Knossos - of which the head has not survived - does not depict a human as was originally thought, but a monkey. The hair of the women is wavy and long, reaching down to the waist. They wear long, multicoloured skirts with flounces, and the upper part of their attire sometimes leaves the breasts exposed. The preference for flowers such as the lily or sea daffodil is typical, and these were subjects particularly favoured in Minoan art. However, the more we examine the details, the more it becomes clear that the art of Akrotiri has its own, local character. The

The original re-construction of the wall painting of the 'Saffron-Gatherer' from Knossos (above) and the recent reconstruction (below).

A duck, ready to fly. This is probably a mallard (*Anas platyrhynchos*).

The fresco of the Antelopes

Here, the artist uses as his ground the same colours as in the wall-painting of the Boxing Boys. A red 'sky' is divided off from the white in the lower part of the wall by an irregular, curving line. Here however, the forms of the animals are not defined by their own colouring, but through a few black lines, with very little additional red for the details of the head. Playing with the thickness of the lines, the artist, with incredible self-assuredness and steadiness of hand, renders not only the plasticity but also all the delicate nature and elegance of the animals. The antelopes are of the species *Oryx beisa*, found in east Africa, and were a favourite subject in Egyptian art. We cannot know whether the Theran artist took his inspiration from Egypt or whether he had actually observed live animals.

subject-matter of the Theran wall-paintings is not that observed on Crete. We discern a more agricultural landscape, rocky rather than coastal; delightful swallows in flight, either single or in pairs, did not occupy the minds of the Minoans. The spirit of the paintings on Thera hints at a religion that was more esoteric, at more individuality of movement, and at an artistic freedom greater than that we perceive in the splendid rituals and official postures of individual figures in Minoan art. The artists here have gone a step further. Their works breathe out a genius of conception and freedom of design. With a few lines, such as in the wall-painting

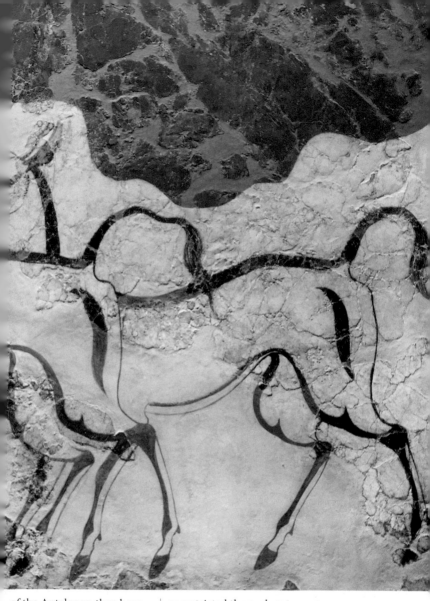

of the Antelopes, they have produced an aesthetic result of unparalleled grace and elegance, touching on the borders of naturalism. Their complete mastery of their subject-matter is also evidenced by the fact that they adapted their compositions perfectly to fit the space available. They either covered whole walls or restricted themselves to those spaces which were created by constructional elements of the buildings, e.g. below built shelves, or between windows, with the area above them enhanced by a band with decorative designs, leaves, spirals or simple straight lines. The Spring fresco was one of the first to be discovered

The fresco of the Antelopes. National Archaeological Museum.

The Spring fresco. National Archaeological Museum.

by excavation, and it is the only wall-painting from Akrotiri to have been found completely in situ. The subject-matter covers three walls of room Δ2, from the floor up to the level where a shelf was fixed. On a beige-cream background a rocky landscape is depicted, with colours very close to those of the volcanic rocks of Santorini. In this wild landscape there grow those most delicate of flowers - lilies - in groups of three, symbolising the regenerative strength of Nature. The lilies cannot help but remind us of those depicted in the villa at Amnisos on Crete, although the flowers here are red, not white. What a huge difference, though, in the nature of the representation! What was an official, almost austere Minoan bouquet pulses with life here, with the stems of the lilies bending in the slight wind. The spring atmosphere is emphasized by the swallows; the artist was not content to show them singly in flight, but he presents them to us in pairs, in one of the most tender and erotic scenes in world art. An eternal poem.

The youthful Boxing Boys are two naked boys who are wearing only belts and have on their right hand a kind of boxing glove, the first to be recorded in the history of athletics. This

Spyridon Marinatos originally believed that the young boxers wore caps, but later on the discovery of the wall-painting with the Saffron-gatherers made it clear that the shorn heads had been painted in a blue colour. The rendering of the anatomical physique of the young boys is worthy of note. It is the oldest known correct representation of children's forms in world art. This fact is of great significance, since even the Greeks of the Classical period depicted children as miniature adults.

type of glove is known from the early historic period and its purpose then was to protect the opponent from dangerous blows. One of the boys wears a necklace, bracelet, and anklet of blue stones, as well as a large gold hoop-earring. Both children have shaven heads, apart from two tresses which hang at the brow and two long plaits at the back.

The 'Flotilla' in the Miniature fresco constitutes the most exciting evidence for shipping in the Aegean area during the Bronze Age, but in more general terms it is a story told in pictures which gives us information of incalculable value. It was found in the spacious room 5 of the West House, developed as a frieze above the windows, while below them there was a band painted to imitate marble. On the left side of the south wall a prosperous city is depicted; a fleet of eight ships is departing from it, and making for another city, to the right; this has a more apparent Minoan character, as can be judged from the sacred horns which decorate the structure depicted, perhaps a peak sanctuary. The houses of both the cities recall those that have been discovered at Akrotiri. They have more than one storey, flat roofs, and are built of ashlar blocks, one next to the other and on different levels. They are also painted in strong colours. The inhabitants can be seen standing at the windows or on the roofs; they are all looking out towards the sea and following the events unfolding there. Behind the left city there is a rocky landscape with the volcanic colours which were so well-known to

the unknown artist; the landscape is enhanced by the presence of plants and animals. In the centre of the picture there is a fleet. We could not imagine a better rendering of a Cycladic fleet during the Bronze Age. This is the first time that we are given an impression of the size of prehistoric ships and such detail of the way they were equipped. The hulls of the ships are painted with birds, fish, and even lions. The prow of each ship is slightly raised and ends in an elegant bowsprit; a man stands in the stern and holds the long rudder, which is single except in two cases. The exactness of this

A war flotilla?
At least some of the passengers on the ships are soldiers; we can clearly make out the helmets hanging on the vessels. The flag decoration on the central ship, however, and the peaceful stances of the passengers and even the dolphins that swim happily between the vessels, present a scene with a peaceful and festive atmosphere. Thus we would like this scene to be one of a marine festival, in honour of some deity unknown to us.

painting solves the problem of the 'ram' which is visible beneath the stern and which, in older representations, led many people to believe that this end of the ship was the prow. Here, it is clear that this is not a ram but a projection which probably helped during embarkation and disembarkation, when the ship approached a sandy beach. Thus during this period, ships transported goods or soldiers and did not engage in manoeuvres designed to ram enemy ships. In the rear of the ship there was a light construction, possibly the cabin of the ship's captain, while the rowers were protected by awnings. The equipment of the ship is shown in every detail. The sail is raised or folded in its place on the deck. The rigging, ropes, flags and standards indicate that this is a particular event. Sometimes, a horizontal boom holds a rectangular sail, and in one case a mast is broken off. Some ships are tied by mooring ropes to bollards on the shore. On the north wall of room 5 there is a scene that is of a pastoral rather than urban nature. It divides into three consecutive levels, giving an impressive example of the prehistoric painter's sense of depth. On the first level, we have a nautical scene with ships and three naked male forms in the water. Some opinions have been voiced that these are swimmers or sponge fishermen, but the strange attitudes of the bodies and the three shields - one for each - that float near them, make it more likely that these are dead soldiers, perhaps the victims of a sea battle. On the second level, on a rocky shore, a row of heavily armed soldiers marches out of a building. They are holding spears

Detail of a representation of a helmet.

and large shields made of animal hides, and wear helmets decorated with rows of boars' tusks; this type of helmet is known to us from Mycenaean tombs. The shafts of the spears are visible behind the shields. On the third level two shepherds, one dressed in a long fleece or skin, lead their flock of sheep and goats towards a pen - in this case an oval enclosure. At its entrance two large trees afford shade during the hot summer days. Nearby, to the left of the entrance, there is a well; this can be concluded from the two water jars that stand on its rim. In front of the well there are some male figures apparently engaged in discussion, while two women who have just filled their water jars are on their way back to the city. One is holding the vessel in her hands and preparing to place it on her head, while the other has already balanced her jar and is walking with a ramrod posture, her hands lowered. Snapshots like these from daily life constitute scenes of unique liveliness, and present a realism which is a departure from the official, formal nature of the Minoan frescoes. The narrow surface areas near the corners of room 5 of the West House

A Fisherman proudly displays his catch. The fish are of the species *Coryphaena hippurus*.

were used by the artist for two scenes that would have been very well-known to the people of the island - two young Fishermen who proudly display their catches. They are naked, their heads shaven except for two short tresses, and they are holding bunches of scomber tied together with thin string. One of the fishermen is shown in the manner usual in very early art, i.e. in profile except for the trunk which is shown *en face*, while the other is rendered completely in profile and with extreme adroitness, given that this was a convention that caused so much difficulty for early artists. The so-called Young Priestess was depicted on another narrow surface between two openings in the same room. The young woman is not wearing the usual Minoan dress with the flounces but a heavy cloak,

probably made of wool.
In room 3A on the first floor of Xeste 3 there were two groups of wall-paintings. The most important figure, the goddess who is none other than the Minoan Mistress of the Animals, was depicted on the north wall. Seated on a tripartite throne, she receives offerings of crocuses from her priestesses and worshippers. The goddess, in front of a landscape with crocuses, is flanked by a griffin and a monkey. Other animals are depicted around her, defining her as the deity who was the

The wall-painting of the Saffron-gatherers.

triple protectoress - of the underworld (chthonic - the snake), the surface of the earth (terrestrial - the monkey) and the air (aerial - the dragonfly). The goddess is an impressive figure. She wears a long flounced skirt and a transparent, open bodice which leaves the breasts uncovered. Her hairstyle and her jewellery are also ornate; she wears a necklace of ducks and dragonflies made of gold and rock crystal, gold earrings, bracelets and a gold diadem, and there is also a cord with gold knots woven into the tresses of her hair. The priestesses/saffron gatherers in the same painting also wear superb garments. On the east wall of the room two of them are depicted amidst a rocky landscape which recalls that of the Spring fresco. For this reason, it is believed that the wall-painting is by the same artist, whose work is characterised by a spontaneity and love of detail in contrast, for example, to that of the artist who painted the Antelopes and placed more emphasis on drawing. The women also wear garments of exquisite taste and delicacy accentuating their femininity and charm, and precious jewellery.

The younger of the two women, on the right, has a shaven head apart from two tresses, and is gathering crocuses with both hands, while the other holds a basket in one hand. This is probably a representation of a ritual, a festival of the Great Mother, to whom there is an altar on which the priestesses are emptying panniers filled with the crocuses

The wall-painting of the Mistress of the Animals. The blue material covering her shoulders is decorated with a line of crocuses.

The crocus is a plant which in all probability originated from Mesopotamia and spread over the countries of the eastern Mediterranean. Saffron was an important luxury ware for centuries in Persia, but as can be judged from the saffron cakes offered by the Phoenicians to the goddess Astarte, and the little metal boxes of saffron found on Egyptian mummies, its religious significance was not lacking. Later on, Cleopatra of Egypt used cosmetics that contained saffron, and the Romans offered wine aromatised with the precious substance at official dinners. In Greece its use is known from the Minoan period, as witnessed by the frescoes of the Saffron-gatherer from the Palace of Knossos on Crete, and the female Saffron-gatherers from Akrotiri. Later on, the creative Greek mind envisaged Krokos as a companion to the god Hermes. One day, when the two friends were playing, Hermes hit Krokos on the head by mistake, and killed him. A plant grew up on the spot, and three drops of his blood fell on the flower, becoming its stigmas, which henceforth bore the name of the unfortunate youth.

Fragment of a wall-painting, with a representation of a crocus.

The wall-painting of the Naked Boys

The pharmaceutical properties of saffron and its uses in cookery and the dyeing of thread made its production very popular throughout antiquity. It is mentioned by Homer, Hippocrates and Pliny. The crocus in the wall-paintings from Santorini and Crete is of the species *Crocus cartwrightianus*, which is endemic to the southern Aegean and grows to this day in Attica, in the Cyclades and on Crete. Centuries of production have created the cultivated crocus (*Crocus sativus*) which is grown commercially only around Kozani. Its cultivation is uncomplicated but its harvesting is an exhausting process; for this reason it is the most expensive of spices. The name saffron for the finished product derives from the Arabic 'zafaran', meaning 'yellow'.

they have gathered. In the room space outside room 3B on the ground floor, there is a representation of a seated man of mature age, wearing a loincloth; three naked boys are advancing towards him. The man and two of the boys are holding vessels, while the third has a piece of cloth. Similar rites are known to us from Egypt, not only from art but also from descriptions. We can therefore conclude that this scene represents an initiation rite; one of the boys has reached manhood and will put on his loincloth for the first time. The water in the vessels was needed for the ritual cleansing that proceeded the initiation.

Crocus cartwrightianus

THE POTTERY

Clay vessels constitute the largest number of portable artefacts found during the excavations. Thousands have already been discovered, and more than fifty different types have been identified. These vessels were either manufactured on the spot or had been imported from regions with which the island inhabitants maintained commercial relations, mainly from Crete but also from mainland Greece, Syria, Palestine etc.

Right: Beaked jug decorated with dark-coloured spirals, the centres of which are outlined in white. Museum of Prehistoric Thera.

Braziers were shallow vessels with a long handle, used to transport lighted charcoals onto which aromatic incense was thrown. They often had a perforated cover through which the smoke could pass. Athens, National Archaeological Museum.

The imported vessels were smaller, for obvious practical reasons, while some pithoi (which normally did not exceed 70cm in height) were themselves used for the transport of smaller vessels stacked inside them, as is the case of the nineteen small Mycenaean 'askoi' that were found inside one pithos. The decoration of the pottery exhibits the characteristics of the respective region from which it originated. With very few exceptions, the vessels from mainland Greece are simpler in form, with geometric decoration such as spirals, wavy lines etc. All the imagination of the Minoan artists is revealed to us on the Cretan vessels of reddish clay with their endless variety of geometric patterns accompanied by schematised flowers, rosettes, spirals etc. As well as the two colours used on the mainland wares (black and red) white is also used, adding tone to the composition and giving

it a lightness. Nor did the painters of the pottery stop there. Although we observe a great variety of decoration inspired by the plant kingdom and can recognise crocuses, myrtle, ivy and capers, it is a curious fact that designs based on the animal kingdom which are frequently seen on pottery in the Minoan centres are absent from the Cretan vessels found at Akrotiri. However, the arrangement of the themes is still zonal, and there remains a preference for the decoration of the upper part of the vessel. The local pottery is more abundant than the imported varieties and consists mainly of vessels for everyday use; it was less carefully produced and decorated than the 'luxury' wares or those vessels which had a religious character. A huge variety of forms can be observed such as pithoi, amphorae, conical rhyta, cups, pithoid amphorae, ewers, cauldrons, braziers for the transport of lighted charcoal and incense, handled cups, and flasks - all of which are found in other parts of Greece - but also nippled ewers, cylindrical vases and strainers, which are typical Cycladic pottery forms. Also worthy of note are the 'kymbes', elongated vessels with handles, which to date have only been found at Akrotiri. They are often decorated with dolphins, swallows or animals which are depicted amidst geometric decoration or the natural environment. The clay used for the Theran pottery is of a light yellowish colour; the colour of the decoration falls into three categories.

Although there is normally an absence of linear decoration on vessels that are less carefully made and intended for everyday use, the find shown here embodies simplicity combined with elegance. Its form is emphasized through the plasticity of vertically orientated 'nerves'. This is a local pottery prototype which must have had cultic use. Athens, National Archaeological Museum.

A double vessel (only one part is preserved) with the representation of crocus flowers and wild goats shown 'at a flying gallop', i.e. with their legs outstretched in opposite directions.
A clay strainer is preserved inside the neck. Athens, National Archaeological Museum.

There are vessels decorated with a matte, dark colour, those which have some details emphasized with white, and finally the polychrome vessels in which the basic brown colour is accompanied not only by white but also by red.

The decoration of the vessels consists of geometric patterns, plant designs such as myrtle leaves, crocuses, ears of corn, lilies, bunches of grapes, and birds or animals such as swallows, storks or cranes, wild goats, felines, and also dolphins. Some of these subjects are limited to a certain type of vessel. It is noteworthy that, although the artists of the time were clearly able to depict the human form, such representations on vessels are a rarity. We can assign vessels with relief decoration to a special category. These are mostly large storage

vessels such as pithoi which have bands of decoration with various linear patterns, added to the vessel after it had taken its final form on the wheel. Relief details seen on smaller vessels such as the 'breasts' or the 'eyes' on various types of jug (nippled ewers, eyed jugs) were also added in this way.

One of the most typical of Cycladic pottery forms is the nippled ewer, a vessel with one handle and an emphasized belly on which two breasts are rendered in relief. The intention of the artist to give the shape of the vessel the abstract form of a female body is also shown in the moulding of the neck, with the spout turned upwards. In some examples, such as the nippled ewer on display in the Museum of Prehistoric Thera, this intention is indicated even more clearly by the 'earrings' that are painted on the upper part of the neck.

Kymbe with painted decoration: on one side, wild goats run amidst rich vegetation, and on the other, there are dolphins. White brush-strokes accentuate the red and brown designs, giving plasticity to the composition. The use to which these vessels were put remains unknown. Athens, National Archaeological Museum.

The strainer jars are typical ceramic forms from Akrotiri, parallel to those which are found on Crete. They have a spherical body and a large, stable base which is cone-shaped, and were used for the preparation of aromatised oils or as incense-burners. They are decorated with spirals, lilies or elegant branches. Athens, National Archaeological Museum.

THE STONE OBJECTS

The hard volcanic rocks of the island such as basalt, trachyte and porphyrite always constituted an ideal raw material, readily available and very durable, for the production of tools and also of vessels. Stone continued to be used in this way throughout the history of the settlement.

A stone hammer which would have had a wooden handle. The grooves for the rope which secured the hammer head to the wooden handle can be seen clearly. Such heavy hammers were probably used for the demolition of ruins after an earthquake. Athens, National Archaeological Museum.

The excavations brought to light a multitude of stone objects such as anvils and hammers of varying sizes (some with a weight of up to 14kg), tools for smoothing and rubbing, millstones and also basins, mortars, palettes for the preparation of colours for plaster, and lamps. Large numbers of stone artefacts with the shape of a four-sided pyramid were found. They probably served as anchors, although another interpretation is that ships' mooring cables were tied to them; a hole in their upper section meant that ropes could be attached. In addition to the objects made of local stone and probably manufactured on the spot, others made of more precious, imported materials such as marble and steatite were

A stone three-legged mill for the grinding of grain. Athens, National Archaeological Museum.

discovered. These were either luxury goods or of a cultic nature (such as rhyta - conical or zoomorphic vessels used in rituals), pyxides (boxes in which cosmetics or jewellery were kept), basins, shallow cups, lamps, drinking cups etc. A square stone seal used to stamp products was also found, and there are some objects made of obsidian, a black, lustrous very hard volcanic glass found only on Melos and used in particular for the production of blades.

Marble basin from Akrotiri. Museum of Prehistoric Thera.

METALWORKING

Metalworking is represented at Akrotiri mainly by bronze objects for everyday use such as vessels of various forms - amphorae, ewers, 'frying pans', large pans, and also knives, saws, sickles, chisels, awls (tools for making holes), and daggers. Two little bronze discs from weighing-scales were also found, as well as a lead cross and lead disc-shaped weights of various sizes which must have been used as weighing standards.

Jewellery and other objects of precious metals such as gold and silver have not been found; this leads to the conclusion that the inhabitants took them away when the settlement was abandoned for good. The wall-paintings certainly indicate that they wore jewellery; the women depicted in them all wear impressive earrings, necklets and bracelets, reflecting the luxury and prosperity exuded by the whole ambience of the settlement.

THE LIFE OF THE INHABITANTS

The finds from the excavations reveal to us a society with a high level of culture. The technical infrastructure (paved streets, underground drainage system) and the careful construction and ornamentation of the houses, along with the luxurious attire of the inhabitants, all bear witness to an urban way of life.

Such an urban centre requires organisation with authorities which would have been responsible for the construction and preservation of public buildings and facilities, the day-to-day administration, and the creation and maintenance of law etc. Unfortunately, we have no information relating to the form of central government or the structuring of society in the prehistoric settlement at Akrotiri. It is not clear whether it was a Minoan colony under the centralised authority of Crete, or whether it enjoyed political autonomy.

Pithos with representations of grapes and grain. Museum of Prehistoric Thera.

However, the economic and cultural autonomy that have been deduced at Akrotiri seem to support the latter premise. To date, no palace or building that would indicate the existence of a central authority has been discovered at Akrotiri; there are only the houses of prosperous townfolk who were not hindered in any way from having direct contact with the Mycenaeans, Evvians of Lefkandi, Thessalians of Iolchos, Trojans etc. Perhaps, therefore, the term 'thalassocracy' which was used by the German historian and archaeologist Fritz Schachermeyer might be the best description for this Theran society, at least as we know it from the present stage of excavations.

Apart from agriculture, the inhabitants were also engaged in animal-keeping and fishing, trade and shipping. They were also accomplished artisans, shipbuilders, builders, potters, woodworkers, workers in metals, and painters. The weaving of cloth was women's work, as is evidenced by the countless loom weights that have been found in the houses; clearly, from the evidence of the wall-paintings, the weaving was preceded by a dyeing process to produce coloured threads. The large number of shells of murex used in the flooring of some rooms indicates that their contents were used widely as a colouring agent. There would also have been a class of people concerned with the administration, and some who had religious duties.

The food eaten by the inhabitants consisted of grains and pulses (actual grains of barley, lentils, chickpeas and millet have been found, as well as depictions of ears of barley and leaves of psychanths on vessels), meat (mainly of sheep and goats, and secondly of pigs - cattle were rare, as they are on the islands today, and perhaps only used for agricultural work), fish, and snails. It is not clear whether saffron, the gathering of which has been attested, was used as a flavouring or simply for its pharmaceutical and colourant properties. Sesame is also attested from carbonised seeds.

Naturally, olives and olive oil could not be missing from the inventory of foodstuffs. The olive tree had already thrived on the island for a long period of time; branches were found in layers of lava beneath the pumice levels. As for the grape, its cultivation is attested by pips which were found on the site and also by its depiction on vessels. Thus we can conclude that its intoxicating end-product was a pleasing accompaniment to the meals of the prehistoric inhabitants of the settlement.

This impressive find of a vessel in which snails were kept indicates to us that the gastronomy of the inhabitants was well developed and included a notable variety of ingredients. Athens, National Archaeological Museum.

RELIGION

The pieces of archaeological evidence relating to the religious beliefs and practices of the inhabitants are very few in number. Just as people would today, when they fled in panic they took with them all the sacred objects linked to their religion, in the hope that they would protect them in the burgeoning catastrophe. Thus we are reduced to hypotheses, based on the knowledge of the religion of neighbouring cultures in the same period, and in particular that of the Minoans.

The wall-painting of the Young Priestess
She is wearing jewellery, and on her shorn head there is a snake. There is no other symbol of priesthood, since the snake was always associated with the chthonic deities. In her hands she holds a brazier, a vessel for the transport of lighted charcoals and incense. This is one of the representations of which the religious character can hardly be doubted.

Religion would have had a pastoral nature; as well as being mystical, soul-stirring and magical, the cycle of vegetation and fruit-bearing was a phenomenon that was important for the survival of the people of the period. They had ascribed the characteristics of the Great Mother, who appears as the wife of the Young God, to this creative force of Nature. The two deities united in a 'sacred marriage', after which the god died, to rise again the following year along with the vegetation. Some researchers have seen this symbolism in wall-paintings such as the Spring fresco, which was found in a place considered by Marinatos to be sacred in view of the discovery of cult vessels in the adjacent room.

To date, the archaeologist's spade has revealed two pieces of evidence for the sacrificial practices of the inhabitants of the settlement. The first is that of two fires dating from the Protocycladic III period, and the second, very near to Xeste 3, that of a sacrifice of hundreds of horned animals, which dates from Late

Cycladic I and was perhaps the last agonised attempt of the inhabitants to attract the help of the gods in the face of burgeoning catastrophe. Certainly the find - carefully protected in a box as a sacred object - of the gold statuette of an ibex which was a sacred animal in the prehistoric Aegean, indicates the relationship of Theran beliefs with those of other religions in the region.

More hints at the beliefs of the inhabitants are provided by the wall-paintings. M. Nilsson, the great expert on religion has said that they "constitute a painted book to which we have to add the text". Certainly Xeste 3, due to the subject-matter of the wall-paintings there and the existence of the 'adyton' with the 'lustral basin' well-known from Crete, was a public shrine. This knowledge helps us in the interpretation of the appearance of the goddess and the ritual offering of crocuses by her priestesses, as well as that of the depiction of the rites of passage to adulthood and the ritual dressing of the boy from room

3B in the same building.
The Miniature Fresco with the flotilla may also have had a religious character. The double horns on the top of the building on the right, the biconcave altar at the lintel of the city gate, the procession of men apparently leading a bull for sacrifice, the men running on the hill - perhaps during some religious games in which a role was played both by the display of oarsmanship depicted immediately below and the presence on the ships of the little cabins or 'ikria' (also found in a separate representation in the wall-painting in Room 4 of the West House) - all add weight to the interpretation of the Miniature fresco as an

is particularly recognisable from the sacred symbols and cultic equipment. This resulted not only from close contacts with the Cretan centres, but can also be ascribed to the presence of Minoans who had established themselves in the settlement. We cannot discern, however, to what degree this Minoan character - in respect of beliefs and religious practices - was influenced by a local element, nor whether it led to the final creation of a separate religion with independent traits, as had happened in the case of Theran art.

Woman with her hand to her face. This scene, which imitates Egyptian prototypes, also appears to relate to a religious ritual of some kind.

important festival.
Finally, reference should be made to the discovery of four sets of double horns of stone in different parts of the settlement. Judging by the Minoan counterparts, these would have had a protective or apotropaic character, especially when they were placed over the entrances to buildings.
On the basis of the information yielded by the excavations to date, we can state that the religion of the inhabitants of Akrotiri had a clear Minoan character which

ANCIENT THERA

In the 9th century BC, Theras and his fugitive comrades arrived from Sparta on the island inhabited by his distant relations who were themselves the descendants of the Phoenicians; he chose to settle on the hill which is known today as Mesa Vouno.

The relief portrait of Artemidorus.

The hill rises to 368 metres above sea level, constituting the second highest point on Santorini. The location is ideal; it is not only a natural fortification which looks out over the whole island, but the two beaches of Oia (modern Kamari) and Elefsina (modern Perissa) which flank it constituted ideal anchorages for ships. Due to its natural fortifications, the city was never surrounded by a wall; the only addition was a little wall which closed off the natural access to it from the north-west side. The Hellenistic and Roman phases of the city have mainly been uncovered, but there are some

The House of Luck. This takes its name from the stature of the goddess Tyche which was found there.

remains of older structures. The excavations in the city and part of the cemetery were conducted from 1895 to 1982 by the German School of Archaeology, and the cemeteries in the NE and NW of Sellada were excavated from 1961 to 1982 by N. Zafeiropoulos.

A VISIT TO THE ARCHAEOLOGICAL SITE

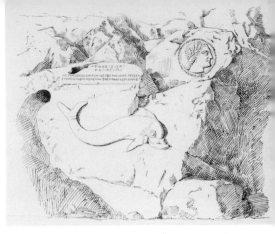

The ancient city, which extends over an area of 300 x 800 metres, has an amphitheatre-like form on long terraces held by retaining walls, opening towards the NE. It is traversed by a central street with small, irregular alleyways running horizontally off it. The entrance to the site is in the NW. On a lower terrace to the east lies the sacred precinct that was founded by Artemidorus of Perge in Asia Minor, who was an admiral in the service of the Ptolemies. As an inscription hewn into the rock informs us, a dream led him to found the sanctuary and dedicate it to various deities which are identified by their symbols chiselled into the rocks as well as by a number of inscriptions. There is the eagle of Zeus, the lion of the garlanded Apollo, the dolphin for Poseidon of the sea. Secondary deities were also worshipped in the sanctuary, such as Omonia, Hekate, the Kaveiroi, Priapos etc. The founder took pains to immortalise himself in a conspicuous location, following a custom popular from the Hellenistic period onwards. We can identify his portrait, in profile and crowned with branches of

The dolphin of Poseidon and the portrait of Artemidorus. From the book 'Thera' by Hiller von Gaertringen.

Left: Vessel from a Theran workshop, from the cemetery of Ancient Thera. Archaeological Museum of Thera.

The Gymnasium. From the book 'Thera' by Hiller von Gaertringen.

The Early Christian church, on the site of the Sanctuary of Pythian Apollo.

bay.
At a right angle to the central road, off to the right, a stone-paved, stepped street leads to the impressive propylon of the Barracks. Built at the highest point of the settlement in a strategic location, this was the seat of the Ptolemaic garrison. It is a building consisting of three tracts of rooms around a four-sided court, with the fourth side corresponding to the entrance. A few metres on from the building there is another edifice with a large, rectangular open court and two rooms on one side of it; this was the Gymnasium of the Barracks, where the soldiers could exercise. Returning to the central street we come to the Agora which, as in all archaic

Greek cities, was the hub of commerce and also of political and social activity. Its central square has a north-south orientation, with a length of 110m and a width that varies between 17 and 30m. The public buildings were located along the west side; the eastern side was partly open, and partly lined with private houses which were of low height and did not obstruct the imposing view. The most majestic of the buildings of the agora was the Royal Stoa, built during the reign of Augustus (1st century AD). It was 46m in length and 10m in width, and its roof was supported on ten Doric columns. On the northern edge of the building there was a place which housed statues of the members of the Imperial family. Around 100 years after it was built the roof collapsed, and it was reconstructed under Antoninus Pius (138-161 AD); its original form was retained. The rostrum at the northern tip was added at that time. In the area behind the Stoa a number of private houses have been excavated which give us a clear impression

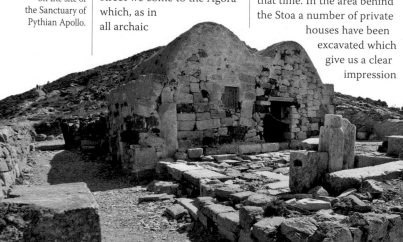

of the dwellings of the ancient inhabitants of Thera. The houses belong to the normal type of Hellenistic dwelling known to us from other ancient Greek cities. The rooms were inward-orientated and developed around a right-angled court - an open space surrounded by a stoa supported on columns which ensured shade in the hot summer months. Below the open space was the cistern, a necessary component of every house, in which rain water was collected. The number of rooms varied in each house according to the economic strength and social standing of its occupants. Many houses had a second floor, as is evidenced by stone staircases which have been found in situ. The main building material was the local limestone. Large hewn ashlar blocks were reserved for the corners of the building, the thresholds of the doorways, the surrounds of the windows and the stairways, while the walls were constructed with small, irregular-shaped stones and covered with plaster. Many of these plastered walls bore painted decoration, but their preservation is so fragmentary that it is impossible to reconstruct the subject-matter.

Proceeding along the central street after the agora, we come to the Hellenistic Theatre on our left, built on the natural slope of the hill. Even if only a small section of the seating is preserved, the perimeter of the orchestra is clear; this was originally circular but - as usual - it was altered during the Roman period to make more space for the stage. The building is impressive for the view it offers rather than for its mode of construction. To the west of the theatre, at a point where an Early Christian church was later built, there was the Sanctuary of Pythian Apollo, and still further west, the Sanctuary of the Egyptian Deities. The worship of Egyptian and other foreign deities was very popular at the end of the Hellenistic period and particularly so during the Roman period; sanctuaries dedicated to them were to be found all over the Greek world. In this sanctuary the deities Isis, Serapis and Anubis were worshipped. Not far

The oldest Greek script was written from right to left in the same way as the Phoenician, and this practice was retained until the beginning of the 6th century BC. Then, for large inscriptions, the Greeks began to use a new form of script: after one row written from left to right, the next row took the opposite direction and the letters were turned round accordingly. This method, which in some parts of Greece -for example Crete - was in use until the end of the 6th century, resembled the way in which a farmer ploughed his field with yoked oxen, and for that reason Pausanias (V.17.6) called it 'boustrophedon'.

of great interest where the history of the Greek script is concerned, because they comprise the oldest form of the Greek alphabet.

On the northern side of the square there is the Sanctuary of Apollo Karneios, which also dates from the 6th century BC. Partly constructed, and partly hewn from the rock, it is entered through a doorway leading to an almost square court beneath which there was a huge cistern to collect rainwater; the roof of the cistern was supported by six large stone pilasters. To the right of the court there was a small, two-roomed building, probably the residence of the priests. To the left there was the temple of Apollo Karneios, which consisted of an anteroom and a cella. On the west wall of the latter two small rooms accessed via steps were probably used as treasuries.

On the opposite side of the square, the Gymnasium of

From the theatre, as from the whole of Ancient Thera, there is a wonderful view out towards the sea.

away, on a lower terrace, there is a little cave that was dedicated to Herakles and Hermes.

The most important and most sacred place in Ancient Thera was located on the SE edge of the city. There is a large square here which was constructed at least as early as the 6th century BC, as is witnessed by its strong retaining walls. The Gymnopaedia, a festival with contests in which young boys participated, was organised in this place from a very early date in honour of Apollo Karneios. Inscriptions which have survived on the smooth rocks of the area are

the Ephebes was built in the 2nd century BC. This was a four-sided building with a large open court which had ancillary rooms on two sides and was used by the young boys for their athletic exercises. Next to the gymnasium, baths were added during the Roman period.

A little further to the south and on a lower terrace there is a cave which was used as a Sanctuary of Hermes and Herakles.

The cemeteries of the city extended over the slopes of Sellada and on both sides of the road that led to its two harbours. Graves dating from the Geometric to the Roman period have been discovered there.

'Gymnopaedia'

As its name indicates*, the Gymnopaedia was a festival celebrated originally by naked boys but later by men in Sparta and other Doric cities, probably from the mid-7th century BC onwards in honour of Apollo, the divine protector of the Dorians. The programme included dances to the sound of odes and hymns of praise, of which the chief composer was Thaletas who is also believed to have founded the festival. During the dances the boys performed gymnastics and with rhythmic movements depicted various forms of contest such as boxing and the 'pancration'. These exercises were part of the programme for the boys' upbringing and their preparation for manhood in order to secure the well-being of the state. An indication of the importance attached to the purpose behind this festival is the fact that when the defeat of Sparta in battle against the Leuktroi (371 BC) was announced in Sparta, the authorities broke off the celebration of the festival. The Gymnopaedia presented a brilliant spectacle of strength, dexterity, suppleness and gracefulness. The spectators at the events readily perpetuated their preference for one or other of the participants in inscriptions - very often with a clearly erotic character - like those that can still be seen, hewn into the rock.

*'Gymnopaedia' derives from the ancient Greek 'gymnos' ('naked'), and 'pais' ('child'), and 'gymnasion' (gymnasium) from the verb 'gymnazein' ('do physical exercise', 'undress for exercise'). Athletics and sports, often with an aesthetic element of dance, were nearly always performed by naked male participants before a male audience.

THE MUSEUM OF PREHISTORIC THERA

This museum in the centre of Fira houses finds from the prehistoric period of the island, mostly from the excavations at Akrotiri, and it is thus one of the most important museums in the country. At present, only some of the wall-paintings that have been discovered are on exhibition, but the collection is continuously being enriched with new material; many new finds are still undergoing conservation.

Fossilized leaves of the olive from the wall of the caldera which have been dated to 60,000 years B.P.

In Room B after the entrance plant fossils, around 60,000 years old and recovered from the walls of the caldera, are on display. The leaves of the olive, palm and lentiscus can be identified. A diagram on the wall of this Room explains the stratigraphy of the caldera.

In Room C there is a typical Cycladic marble figurine dating from the Protocycladic II period (2700-2400 BC), as well as other Protocycladic marble figurines and artefacts from Akrotiri and the cemetery in the Fira quarry. There is also a large marble basin from Akrotiri and there are vessels from the north-east Aegean (a 'depas amphikypello' or type of drinking vessel, one or two-lugged cups, a flask, globular jugs etc). These vessels are undisputed evidence of the contacts between the prehistoric inhabitants of the island and the great centres of the Bronze Age, and it is possible that the abandonment of these centres, such as Poliochni on Lemnos and Thermi on Lesvos, favoured the great development of Akrotiri into a commercial hub.

In the same showcase, there are two nippled ewers with superbly realistic representations of swallows in flight.

In Room D, a plan on the wall and a model give us a clear impression of the archaeological site of Akrotiri. In Room D1 there are the plaster casts of an ornate table with three legs and of a section of a chair, and in another showcase there

Nippled ewer decorated with swallows. End of the 18th century BC.

are three tripod cauldrons, a portable clay oven and a pair of supports for little 'souvles' (grilling sticks) with zoomorphic terminals. The well-preserved imprint of a basket is also of interest here. Amongst the bronze implements in the same Room: a censer, large pans, parts of a weighing-scales, a dagger closely resembling those found in the royal graves at Mycenae, fire tongs for raking over charcoals, a large saw and the nozzle of some metallurgical bellows. Nearby, there is a clay bathtub from Akrotiri; like similar examples found on Crete it is of small dimensions - the people at that time obviously bathed in a seated position. In the bottom there is a hole for the water to flow out and in the rim there are two handles with holes for ropes, to make transport easier.

The existence of such bathtubs bears witness to the high cultural level of the inhabitants, especially when we remember that palaces built more than 3,000 years later, such as that at Versailles, did not have bathrooms at all!

In Room D2 there are standardised lead weights, from a few grammes to 15kg, which are multiples or submultiples

Portable clay oven. 17th century BC.

Left: an 'asaminthos' (bathtub). 17th century BC.

Pair of grill supports with zoomorphic terminals. 17th century BC.

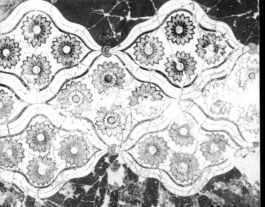

Sherds bearing Linear A script.

The wall-painting with the relief rosettes.

of the metric units that were used on Crete. In the same showcase there are fragments of Linear A script, the Cretan-Minoan script which has not yet been deciphered. The drawings on the three large pithoi in the same Room are probably indicative of what they once contained e.g.water in the case of the pithos bearing a design of rushes. In another showcase there are clay seal impressions, as well as stone and clay stamp-seals.

The right-hand showcase in Room D3 is dedicated to the materials that were found at Akrotiri. Vessels which still contain ancient lime-plaster or red colour and other pigment materials bring us close to the prehistoric creators of the superb wall-paintings that have been discovered in the settlement. In the remaining part of the Room we are given an impression of the wall-paintings which decorated the houses at Akrotiri during the periods preceding that of the final catastrophe. It is an impressive fact that older layers of wall-paintings were found in nearly all of the houses; this indicates that the inhabitants had chosen painting at a very early date as the medium for the decoration of their homes, and also explains the enormous dexterity of

The wall-painting with the sea daffodils (*Pancratium maritimum*). These plants were previously identified as papyrus (*Cyperus papyrus*).

the artists in the rendering of their subject-matter; it resulted from the development of a tradition over a long period. The subject-matter which has been brought to light to date is decorative, on the one hand naturalistic, and on the other a combination of relief with painting. It is a technique well-known from Crete. In the centre of the Room there is an ornate three-legged offertory table.

Room D4 features a reconstruction of part of the House of the Ladies. Three walls of a room are decorated with large sea daffodil plants (previously identified as papyrus) in a rather stylised composition, one beside the other and each with three flowers. Sections of painting with representations of women have been preserved from two other walls; the figures are depicted on a white background.

The upper part of the wall, separated from the scene with the figures through an undulating, curved line, contains a pattern of rhomboid shapes with stars and has been interpreted as a stylised, starry sky. The bare-breasted figure holds a piece of material and offers it to a third woman of whom only the lower part of her clothing is preserved. The scene could represent a ritual dressing ceremony, analogous to that of the naked boy, or it may depict preparations for a marriage ritual. On the adjacent wall there are fragments of wall-paintings that yield information about the flora of the island. Chaste tree, rushes, crocuses, and myrtle are some of the plants that were well-known to the inhabitants of ancient Akrotiri. There is even a dragonfly hovering amongst the plants, a humble insect which nevertheless aroused the interest of the unknown painter.

In front of the wall opposite there are two cylindrical pithoi, one with a representation

The use of stamp-seals was discovered at a very early date as a method of indicating the authenticity, ownership or origin of an article. The practical need for every seal to have a different design in order to make it unique led to the creation of a whole new chapter of art which - if nothing else - stands out for the variety and imagination of its creators. Beginning with simple geometric designs, it progressed to include representations of animals, gods, and also complete scenes involving several figures. Minoan and Mycenaean art have yielded little masterpieces in this sphere. Sealstones were often made of semi-precious stones or precious metals and would have been taken away by the inhabitants of Akrotiri when they abandoned the settlement. The impression was stamped into a lump of clay and bound to the object it related to with a piece of twine. The seals on display here are most likely of Cretan clay with typical Minoan representations (bulls, chariot races, griffins, groups of animals), and probably accompanied imported goods.

Kymbe with ibex and dolphins. 17th century BC.

Rhyton in the form of a bull. 17th century BC.

Cylindrical pithos with dolphins. 17th century BC.

Museum of Prehistoric Thera
Fira
Open daily except Mondays

of dolphins against a light-coloured background, and the other of white lilies on a dark background, analogous to vessels which have been found on Crete.

In the next Room there are vessels which were of practical and ritual use. In the right hand corner there are zoomorphic rhyta in the form of a lion's head, or of a wild boar, and in the left-hand corner there is a vessel in the form of a triton shell (photos). Also of interest are the nippled ewers, a vessel decorated with representations of cultivated plants (among them a vine bearing grapes), and a pithoid amphora with a representation of an eagle on it.

In Room D7 there are vessels imported from Aegina, mainland Greece, Kos, Naxos, Kea, Crete and also from the rest of the eastern Mediterranean, indicating the regions with which the inhabitants of Akrotiri had contacts.

From the northern area of the settlement that has been excavated to date there are the fragments of the wall-paintings with the head of an African, the Blue Bird and the Adorant Monkeys. The latter fragment depicts a shrine, of which one column with two papyrus flowers is preserved. On top of the column there are the sacred double horns on a stepped base, while in front of the shrine two monkeys sit with their arms raised in a posture of worship.

Room D7 (2) is dominated by the wall-painting of the Blue Monkeys, which originated from room 6 of Building B. Above a blue wavy base which is perhaps intended to represent the sea, there is a rocky landscape with the well-known colours of Santorini. Blue monkeys climb over the rocks in an impressive variety of poses which, in addition to the artist's ability to

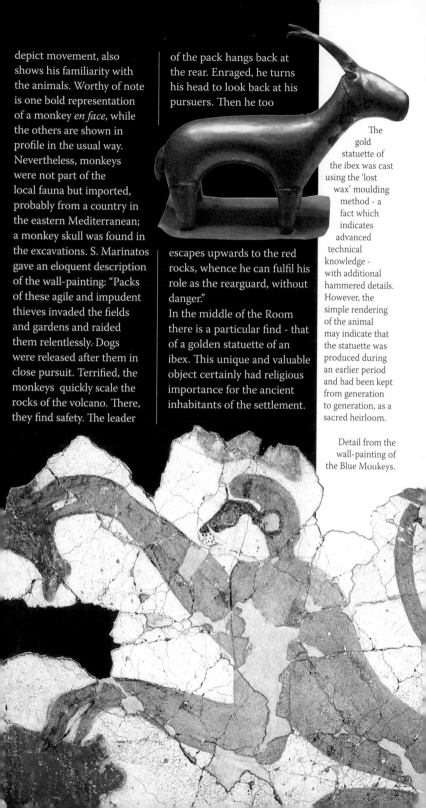

depict movement, also shows his familiarity with the animals. Worthy of note is one bold representation of a monkey *en face*, while the others are shown in profile in the usual way. Nevertheless, monkeys were not part of the local fauna but imported, probably from a country in the eastern Mediterranean; a monkey skull was found in the excavations. S. Marinatos gave an eloquent description of the wall-painting: "Packs of these agile and impudent thieves invaded the fields and gardens and raided them relentlessly. Dogs were released after them in close pursuit. Terrified, the monkeys quickly scale the rocks of the volcano. There, they find safety. The leader

of the pack hangs back at the rear. Enraged, he turns his head to look back at his pursuers. Then he too escapes upwards to the red rocks, whence he can fulfil his role as the rearguard, without danger."

In the middle of the Room there is a particular find - that of a golden statuette of an ibex. This unique and valuable object certainly had religious importance for the ancient inhabitants of the settlement.

The gold statuette of the ibex was cast using the 'lost wax' moulding method - a fact which indicates advanced technical knowledge - with additional hammered details. However, the simple rendering of the animal may indicate that the statuette was produced during an earlier period and had been kept from generation to generation, as a sacred heirloom.

Detail from the wall-painting of the Blue Monkeys.

THE ARCHAEOLOGICAL MUSEUM OF THERA

This museum, located in the centre of Fira near to the cable car station, is housed in a building which in 1960 replaced one that had been destroyed by the earthquake of 1956. It contains finds that cover the history of the island from the prehistoric to the Roman period.

In the first room there are prehistoric vessels from Akrotiri, both of local and of Minoan origin. Of particular interest is an unpainted vessel with relief spirals which recalls a similar one in the National Archaeological Museum. In a special showcase there is a clay daedalic figurine of a mourner. The figure wears a deep red chiton belted in the middle and has one hand to the head while the other tears at the hair; this is a posture known to represent that of a mourner. The figurine originates from the cemetery of Ancient Thera. The room is otherwise dominated by the marble torsos of archaic kouroi, one of which originates from the shrine of Apollo Karneios on Ancient Thera.

Geometric art is well represented in the museum in vessels that originate mainly from the cemetery of Ancient Thera. One showcase is dedicated to finds from the sanctuary of Aphrodite on Ancient Thera and contains female statuettes of marble or clay, others in the form of animals, and vessels of various shapes which constituted offerings or were used in rites in honour of the goddess.

The marble head of a kouros, dating from the end of the 6th century BC, originates from the agora of Ancient Thera. A large amphora with relief decoration, dating from the 7th century BC, is of interest. On the neck there is the representation of a swan and on the body of the vessel there are winged horses drawing a chariot. This product of a Cycladic workshop was found in the

Torso of a kouros from Ancient Thera. Second half of the 6th century BC.

Archaeological Museum of Thera
Fira
Open daily except Mondays

black-painted vessels and Attic red-figured wares dating from the mid-5th century BC, and a pelike of the Kerch style (4th century BC).

Another showcase contains kernoi (very simple vessels to contain seed offerings), male figurines, and zoomorphic vessels (bird, horse, ram, dolphin, and monkey) for cultic use.

The last section of the room mainly contains sculptures of the Late Hellenistic and Roman periods from ancient Thera, including the sculpted heads of young men from the Ptolemaic Gymnasium, a sculpted head (perhaps of Aphrodite) from the Royal Stoa, and part of a funeral stele on which the head of a woman is depicted, dating from the end of the 5th century BC.

cemetery of Ancient Thera. The same cemetery yielded the funerary kouros (extensively destroyed) dating from the second half of the 7th century BC. The marble lion (c.600 BC) stood in the agora of the city.

The next showcases contain Attic black-figure wares, notable among them an amphora depicting on one side Athena and Herakles in a four-horse chariot (quadriga) and Apollo and Artemis in a separate scene, and on the other two horses standing between an archer and a hoplite. There are also

Left: head of an archaic kore from Ancient Thera. End of the 6th century BC.

Clay statuette of daedalic type depicting a mourner, from the cemetery of Sellada.

The Megaron Gysi Cultural Centre

Woman's folk costume from Santorini.

This is housed in a 17th century mansion of particular architectural interest in Fira town. Part of the building survived the earthquake of 1956 and was restored under the supervision of the Catholic bishopric of Thera. The careful restoration is apparent in all of the main and ancillary rooms of the building which today is used for cultural events. The permanent exhibition contains etchings from the 16th to the 19th centuries which depict local folk costumes, landscape paintings and drawings, maps, manuscripts and photographs of the island before the earthquake, as well as paintings by great artists who have worked on Santorini. Since 1981 the Cultural Centre has organised a Festival of Artistic Events every August with music concerts and exhibitions of art, to which entry is free for visitors.

The open space around which the ground-level rooms of the Foundation are arranged.

The Dominican Nunnery of St. Catherine

Gysi Cultural Centre / Fira
Open 1st May - 31st October
Monday - Saturday: 10.00 - 16.00
Closed on Sundays

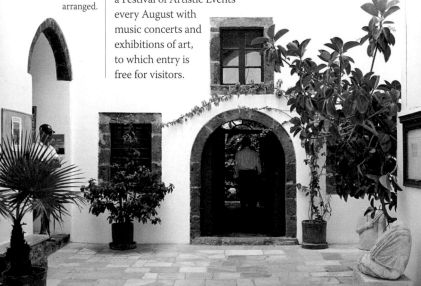

'Petros M. Nomikos' Conference Centre

Located in Firostefani, the Centre is housed in a beautiful, renovated Neoclassical mansion whence there is a view out over the caldera. Apart from its publications and the numerous events that are organised there on the theme of Aegean Culture, the Centre offers the visitor the unique opportunity to see at close range all of the wall-paintings that have been found at Akrotiri. In the impressive underground tunnels of the centre, there are exact, three-dimensional reproductions of the paintings, produced using state-of-the-art technical methods. The exhibition is enhanced by a great number of informative posters and photographs of the excavation work.

The impressive underground tunnels that house the exhibition of wall-paintings from Akrotiri.

Comprehensive information is provided beside each wall-painting.

Petros M. Nomikos Conference Centre
Firostefani
Tel. +30 22860 23016

Koutsouyiannopoulos Wine Museum

Wine Museum
Vothonas
Open
April - November
Daily
12.00 - 20.00
November - March
Daily
09.00 - 14.30
Closed on Sundays

The Wine Museum in the place called Vothonas, on the road to Kamari, is the only underground wine museum in Greece. It lies 6 metres below the surface and is 300 metres in length. It contains models that give visitors a vivid impression of the wine-making activity on the island from 1660 to 1970, as well as the tools and equipment related to it.

The guided tour is automated; as the visitor passes each point mechanisms are activated which work through photocells and initiate movement linked with sound, in presentations relating to the cycle of wine production. Particularly impressive is the space itself in which the museum is housed; it is the largest tunnel on Santorini.

Pyrgos Ecclesiastical Collection

The Pyrgos Ecclesiastical Collection is housed in the restored Catholic church of Ayia Triada, next to the church of the Presentation of the Virgin Mary. It comprises icons, woodcarvings, vestments, and ecclesiastical equipment, mostly dating from the 16th and 17th centuries when Pyrgos enjoyed its greatest prosperity. Particularly noteworthy is an icon of St. George, dating from the 15th century.

The icon of St. George.

Theotokaki, as the church of the Assumption of the Virgin is affectionately known, dates from the 10th century and is believed to be the oldest church on Santorini. It is located within the precinct of the castle of Pyrgos near to Ayia Triada, and is famed for its wood-carved iconostasis and its icons. The church can only be visited on a few days in August when the festival of the Assumption is celebrated.

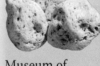

Museum of minerals and fossils

This museum is located in Perissa and was founded in 2006 by the Cultural Society of Thera. It contains rocks and fossils from Santorini and abroad.

Typical 'living-room' of a Santorini 'cave' house. Everything is arranged with order and taste.

Emm. Lignos Folk Museum

This museum was founded in Kodohori, Fira by lawyer, journalist and director of the newspaper 'Theraïka Nea' Emmanuel Lignos. It is housed in a typical, two-room 'cave' house which was built in 1861, survived the earthquakes, and was restored and preserved in 1973. In 1993 a new wing was added to house the Art Gallery and the workshops, as well as the little chapel of Ayios Konstantinos. The museum contains furniture, utensils, costumes and tools as well as an historic archive. The works of well-known artists are on display in the gallery.

Picture from the printing workshop. The hand-operated press can be seen.

Emm. Lignos Folk Museum
Kodohori
Open daily
19.00-14.00
& 18.00-20.00

Oia Nautical Museum

Where shipping was concerned, Santorini reached the zenith of its prosperity during the 19th century, when the demand for Theran earth and its quality wines gave exports a tremendous boost. Ships from Santorini plied the whole Mediterranean, trading in the island products and bringing back other goods, and wealth, to the island. All of this activity is presented in a very pictorial way in the Oia Nautical Museum, which was founded in 1951 by Captain Antonis Dakoronias and is housed today in a captain's residence dating from the 19th century. Through the museum all of the island's nautical adventure is relived, not only its wealth but also the toil and sweat of the ships' crews which contributed to the creation of such prosperity. There are watercolours and models of ships, maps, logbooks and other documents, tools, and flags as well as a plethora of small exhibits relating to the life of the sailors.

Oia Nautical Museum
Oia
Open daily except for Tuesdays
10,00 - 14.00 and 17.00 - 20.00

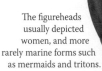

The figureheads usually depicted women, and more rarely marine forms such as mermaids and tritons.

MAPS OF THE AEGEAN

The Greek archipelago - both the land and the sea lapping it - has always been a place for the meeting and interaction of prehistoric and historic societies, and thus a much-frequented region. The seaways which link the great trading centres of the region with one another pass through the Aegean, from the Black Sea to Egypt and the Near East on the one hand and to the western Mediterranean on the other. Throughout their long history, the harbours of the islands have welcomed ships laden with goods, warriors, pilgrims, pirates, scholars, and those seeking their fortune. Shipping created the need to compile maps for the use of those who embarked on journeys that were perilous not only because of the prevailing local weather conditions, but also because of political considerations. Although the ancient nautical charts themselves have not survived, the 'periploes' - works which describe sea routes and distances - presuppose their existence. Ancient traditions formed the basis for some Byzantine 'periploes' such as the 'Stadiodromon', a text preserved in the work of Konstantinos Porphyrogenitos which refers to the distances between the ports of call of the Imperial fleet when an attempt was to be made to capture Crete from the Arabs in 949 AD. Sailing from Constantinople, the fleet was to pass through the Hellespont and reach Crete via the islands of Tenedos, Lesvos, Chios, Samos, Naxos and Thera. The nature of the information provided by such works (which were accompanied by the relevant maps), is revealed to us in another Byzantine text: "...which winds move the sea and which winds blow from the land; so that they will recognise the hidden rocks in the sea, the places where it is of no depth, and the land that lies beside it, and know how great the distance is from one harbour to another..." The inadequate knowledge of the Middle Ages has left us pictures of the world rather than maps. In the 12th century the Arab geographer Edrizi undertook the mapping of the Aegean, but we owe the first maps of the Archipelago itself to the 15th century Florentine humanist and priest Christoforo Buondelmonti. His work created a great sensation and was followed up by many historians and geographers. Thus from his maps (*portolani*) we progress to the *isolarii*, books with maps and descriptions as well as historical or

Santorini and the Christiana Islands from the Insularium of Marco Boschini, '*L'Arcipelago*', Venice 1658.

cultural information about the islands. Such texts relating to the islands of the Aegean were also written by Bartholomeo da li Sonetti, Benedetto Bordone, Francesco Piacenza, Olfert Dapper, Pitton de Tournefort and - most important of all - the Venetian cosmographer Vincenzo Coronelli.

From the ISOLARIO of Antonio Millo

"*Santorini is an island which, as if risen from the sea, appears to be snow-covered. It is well provided with strongholds (kastri), one on the west side (ponente) which is called Skaros and has the largest number of inhabitants since it is near the port, one on the east side (grego) which is called Akrotiri, and another (sirocco levante) called Apanomeria. The port is on the west side (ponente), but it is for small boats and galleys; the anchorage of this harbour lies between the island of Santorini and the reef of Kaimeni which you could say was born in recent years. Not only that, but from '70 to '75 the sea spouted fire 3 miles away from this reef and a large raft of pumice was created - out on the sea, like a ship. I saw this for certain. On the west side of the island there is Therasia, which they say was inhabited in the olden days and joined to Santorini. A little distance away from that is the reef of Aspronisi. Santorini has only one harbour in the east, an anchorage called Akri. From there to Christiana in the south west it is a distance of 18 miles. From the latter island, Crete lies 80 miles to the south.*
The perimeter of Santorini measures 40 miles."

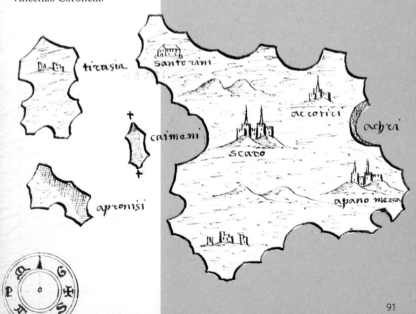

M.G.F.A. de Choiseul-Gouffier, *Voyage pittoresque de la Grèce, Paris 1782.*

"The island of Thera, modern Santorini, has always been the theatre for the most interesting of phenomena. At this point in the Archipelago, it looks as if Mother Nature has merged together - under the gaze of the observer - a series of differing processes which, open to free interpretation, appear to reveal her secrets."

Oia in a drawing by M.G.F.A. de Choiseul-Gouffier.

Gustave Fougères, *Grèce, 1911.*

"From the harbour (Skala), narrow but much sheltered from the north wind, we went up (20', donkey 1 drachma), following a path on a zig-zag which had a supporting parapet wall along its whole length, and little gulleys and houses hewn out of the black tufa, until we reached the top of the rock (at a height of 205 metres) which is crowned by the domes and white houses of Fira."

Map of Santorini (1745) by the Russian monk and traveller Vasili Gregorovitch Barsky.

Philip Sanford Marden, *Greece and the Aegean Islands, Boston-N. York 1907*
"Historically, Thera has enjoyed little renown when compared to the other islands. But our opinion is that it excels them all in other qualitative characteristics. It seems that myth has not honoured the island as it should, and poetry has not sung its praises. No Byron has filled his cup with Santorini wine. No hot-blooded poetess has lived and sung in its winding alleyways. No Olympian god has asserted that he was born here. But where beauty of all kinds is concerned - from pastoral to majestically awesome -Thera has no equal in the Aegean."

The harbour at Fira in a photograph by Fougères and Merle (1902).

Nelly's, Recollections from Santorini.
"I will never forget that enchanting picture presented by the face of the island. It felt as if I was looking at a huge chocolate cake, garnished with cream. When the sun rose and cast its golden rays over the island, I could not look my fill. I have never seen such a sight; I try to avail myself of those unforgettable moments once again, and to immortalise them, through the photos that I took there."

An inhabitant of Santorini in a coloured copperplate etching by Jacques Crasset de Saint Sauveur.

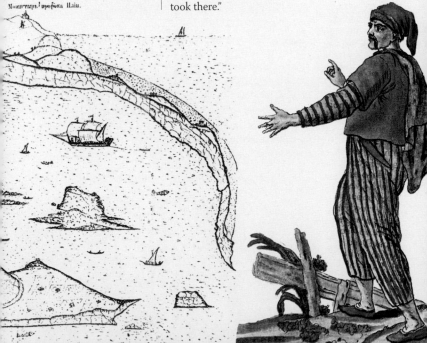

THE VILLAGES

Santorini has a permanent population of 13,600, distributed amongst 13 villages. Before the terrible earthquake of 1956 the number of inhabitants was much larger but the huge damage that was caused to the houses, coupled with the fear that the catastrophe would be repeated, forced many people to leave the island.

Fira

Art is ever-present. There are many galleries on Santorini.

Opposite page: Fira. The Orthodox metropolitan church of Ipapantis dominates up on the rim of the caldera.

Fira is the capital of the island and thus the place where the visitor can find all essential services: a health centre, chemists, banks, a police station, car and motorcycle rentals, shops etc. Also located there is the cable car station which connects the town with the old port from which caiques make the trips to the Kammeni islands and Therasia. To return up to the town from the port, the visitor can choose between the cable car, a donkey, or - when of an athletic constitution - ascend to the town via the winding, stepped pathway. The activity within the town generates an unavoidable hectic. Nevertheless, its situation is superb and the western side of it continues to be of architectural

interest. A stroll through its narrow little alleys, a cup of coffee or a meal with a view out towards the arresting landscape of the volcano, are all definitely worthwhile.

The donkeys are the 'taxis' of Fira from the little harbour to the town and provide an alternative to the cable car.

Firostefani is the continuation of Fira northwards and offers a wonderful view out over the caldera. There are a number of exquisite hotels here, and houses that are impressive and colourful.

Above left: The rock of Skaros with the remains of the castle on top.

Imerovigli

Imerovigli is located at the highest point on the cliffs of the caldera, 385 metres above sea level. The greater part of the settlement was destroyed in 1956 and abandoned by the inhabitants. Thus today, most of the buildings that have been reconstructed are rented out as holiday accomodation, many with high specifications. Visitors can walk around the remains of the medieval (Frankish) settlement of Skaros with its Catholic monastery of Panayia tou Rosariou.

A little alleyway in Imerovigl. The walk up from Fira to this point an experienc without paralle

In Imerovigli, as in all of the other villages of the island, visitors never tire of taking photographs.

Imerovigli as seen from Firostefani

Oia

Undoubtedly the most beautiful village on Santorini, combining the majestic landscape of the caldera with architecture of a high aesthetic and a more moderate degree of tourist development. The houses, built on different levels, lie far enough away from the central, marble-paved commercial street and offer an ideal refuge for visitors who love peace and quiet. Two sets of steps lead to the little harbours of Ammoudi and Armeni, where visitors can swim or enjoy local food in the picturesque tavernas. At the northern edge of the village there are the remains of the castle of Ayios Nikolaos; this is a place to enjoy an unforgettable sunset. The only disadvantage is that all visitors to the island have the same intention…
In Oia, a visit can be made to the Nautical Museum, and to a traditional weaver's workshop to watch the local way of weaving.

Ayios Loukas, the most photographed church on Santorini

Opposite page:
The flowering bougainvillea blends harmoniously with the architecture of Oia.

A panoramic view of Oia from the castle of Ayios Nikolaos.

Ayii Apostoli. The blue of the bell-tower merges with the blue of the sky.

The castle at Pyrgos. The churches of Theotokaki (left), Ayia Triada (right) and the Presentation of the Virgin Mary (background right) are to be seen.

Panayia Kasteliou

Pyrgos

Built high on a hill with an unlimited view out over the whole of Santorini, Pyrgos was a typical Cycladic fortified village which developed during the Venetian period around a 'kastelli' - a castle which was destroyed by the earthquake of 1956. Simple houses and mansions, narrow alleyways with steps and passages to save space, and more than 40 churches transport us to an environment of a kind which - unfortunately - has become very rare today. Of the churches, the most noteworthy are Theotokaki, built in the 10th century and containing icons of the 16th and 17th centuries and a carved wooden iconostasis,

the cave church of Ayios Nikolaos of Kisera, and the church of the Presentation of the Virgin or Panayia Kasteliou (17th century), whence at Easter the picturesque procession of the Epitafion, in the light of tin lamps, proceeds through the whole village.

Mesaria

Located on a crossroads at the centre of the island, Mesaria was once a village of great commercial enterprise. The ruins of the Markezinis knitting factory are still extant, as well as many mansions and 'cave' houses; there are also numerous churches such as those of Ayia Irini and Ayios Dimitrios, at which great festivals are held.

Vothonas

Vothonas does not offer impressive views like other villages of Santorini but it constitutes a very interesting example of a village built along the course of a ravine, for protection against pirate attack. The inhabitants' cave houses and the narrow alleyways create an architectural complex which will not disappoint those who have the time to visit this village, far from the tourist centres of the island.

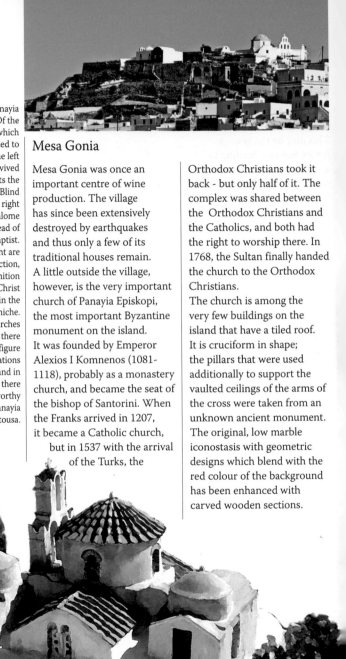

Church of Panayia Episkopi. Of the frescoes, which have been dated to around 1100, the left tract has survived and depicts the Healing of the Blind Man. The right tract shows Salome holding the head of St. John the Baptist. Also on the right are the Resurrection, and the Dormition of the Virgin. Christ is depicted in the shallow niche. Beneath the arches of the vaults there are also full-figure representations of saints, and in an annexe there is a noteworthy icon of Panayia Vrefokratousa.

Mesa Gonia

Mesa Gonia was once an important centre of wine production. The village has since been extensively destroyed by earthquakes and thus only a few of its traditional houses remain. A little outside the village, however, is the very important church of Panayia Episkopi, the most important Byzantine monument on the island. It was founded by Emperor Alexios I Komnenos (1081-1118), probably as a monastery church, and became the seat of the bishop of Santorini. When the Franks arrived in 1207, it became a Catholic church, but in 1537 with the arrival of the Turks, the Orthodox Christians took it back - but only half of it. The complex was shared between the Orthodox Christians and the Catholics, and both had the right to worship there. In 1768, the Sultan finally handed the church to the Orthodox Christians.

The church is among the very few buildings on the island that have a tiled roof. It is cruciform in shape; the pillars that were used additionally to support the vaulted ceilings of the arms of the cross were taken from an unknown ancient monument. The original, low marble iconostasis with geometric designs which blend with the red colour of the background has been enhanced with carved wooden sections.

Emborios

Emborios or Emborio is one of the largest villages on Santorini and was the commercial centre ('emborio') of the island. This may be the reason for its name; according to another view the name is a corruption of the German 'Neuburg', which means 'new castle' and relates to the rectangular medieval fortress preserved there to this day. Above its entrance there is a slot from which boiling oil could be poured down on attackers. At the village entrance there is the little church of Ayios Nikolaos Marmaritis, built on the site of a sanctuary of Hellenistic date. On the nearby hill of Gavrilos, on which Byzantine remains are scattered, there are eight 19th century windmills, preserved as monuments of a bygone age.

The windmills of Emborio, as they were around 1900.

The 'gulas' (castle) of Emborio.

Kamari and Perissa are two very well-known villages today, but they were actually created during recent decades as a result of the tourist development on the island, and on account of their long, sandy beaches. There is nothing of architectural interest there, but they are places for those who wish to add water sports and nightlife to their stay.

THE BEACHES

Santorini is endowed with many places where visitors can enjoy the clear, deep blue Aegean waters. There is a choice between beaches on the 'inside', western shore of the island which looks towards the caldera, and the 'outside' eastern shore looking out to the open sea. The western shore offers very small beaches, such as at Armeni, or the opportunity to dive from the rocks, such as at Ammoudi and the little island of Ayios Nikolaos below Oia, and also the chance to experience a deep, almost bottomless sea as terrifying as it is unique. The outside shore of the island consists of endless beaches with white or - more often - black sand of volcanic origin. In general, the beaches in the south of the island, such as those at Kamari, Perissa, Perivolos or Red Beach, are the most frequented, while those in the north, such as at Koloumbos and Baxedes, are more for those who wish to escape the crowds.

Ammoudi

Red Beach

Kamari

TRADITION

THE ARCHITECTURE

Environmental conditions such as the blinding light, strong winds, lack of water and wood but contrastingly infinite supply of stone on the one hand, and the frequent earthquakes on the other, are the parameters which have defined the architecture and shape of the village settlements. Their alignment parallel to the curve and sweep of the island's topography leads to the creation of an aesthetically pleasing, irregular network of structures, in a balanced relationship with the landscape.

In general terms, the architecture of Santorini has many elements in common with that of the other Cycladic islands. There are, however, building forms peculiar to the island that are worthy of study.

The settlements can be divided into three categories: a) fortified, such as those at Pyrgos, Emborio and Akrotiri, created by building activity outside and around the walls of a castle, b) linear, such as those at Fira and Oia which have developed along the rim of the caldera, and c) those such as Finikia, Vothonas and Karterados in which the houses normally follow the course of a natural ravine and are hewn into the vertical face of the layer of aspa. In actual fact there are villages of mixed type, with buildings belonging to one or more of the above categories.

As far as the method of construction of the houses is concerned, there are three types: a) built, b) cave houses ('iposkafa'), c) semi-

built. The first category is completely built on a level surface, the second hewn into the layer of aspa, and the third is part built, part hewn out of the aspa. In particular, the strong slope of the ground and the possibility of hewing out and making new rooms beneath the overlying house has led to a unique freedom of expression. The buildings are often in such close proximity that it is difficult to discern where one ends and the next begins, and the irregular bulks of the houses form a sculpted entity.

The main building materials are of local, volcanic origin. Imported materials are sparingly used and only when absolutely necessary - e.g. wood for doors and windows and iron for the reinforcement of the skylights. The materials which the island yields its inhabitants and with which, through their own aesthetic, they have created a huge variety of forms and designs and thus turned simple utility spaces into

sculptures of artistic merit, are the following: 1) black stone, a very hard material used for supporting walls and enclosure walls, 2) red stone of compact, hard type used for pillars, lintels and additions to the outside walls, or red stone of porous type used for the construction of vaulted roofs, 3) pumice, for the construction of domes, and 4) 'aspa' - Theran earth or 'pozzuolana'. The latter is volcanic tephra, the most important building material because it is easily hewn; the famous cave houses of Santorini have been gouged out of the natural aspa layer. Also, when mixed with lime, it produces a

very durable cement with hydraulic properties, used for the insulation of cisterns for water and also for the construction of domes without the need for reinforcement with iron. The cave houses and the domes constitute the two basic, special characteristics of the island architecture. The vault of the dome, which is always visible inside the house and may be semi-cylindrical, boat-shaped or cruciform, can either retain its form externally or be covered over by a flat surface which for practical reasons is often accessible.

As for their actual method of construction, the houses are of the cave ('iposkafa') type, built, or a mixture of the two, with some rooms hewn from the aspa and others built in the normal way.

The houses are normally small and have narrow facades with the rooms extending backwards behind them. The façade has a door with two windows positioned symmetrically on each side of it. Above the door is a kind of skylight, a third window with an arched or straight top lintel. Behind the façade is the main room of the house, with the bedroom behind that. The wall which separates the two rooms repeats the form of the façade with its four openings. In some houses there is a third room even further behind; this is dark

A typical Santorini cave house

Oia. Town planning on the brow of the caldera.

and because of its irregular shape, is called a 'cave'. A house can be limited to this simple plan, or there may be more rooms to the left or right, an upper floor (rare), or other additional rooms. The usual ancillary rooms (kitchen, toilet) were traditionally located outside the main house and accessed from the courtyard in which there was also a built oven - a useful and elegant component of the house. However, for both permanent residents and visitors the needs of modern living have led to architectural interventions and the incorporation of these ancillary rooms into the main built complex.

All of the houses have an underground water storage tank (cistern), in which rain water is collected; it can be directly under the house, but is more usually beneath the courtyard. In some agricultural villages every house has a '*kanava*', a place for the production and storage of wine.

In contrast to the normal

For the construction of a dome, the wooden moulding is supported on wooden joists of varying height which follow the outline of the half-circle. The space between the joists is covered with transverse wooden planks on top of which a layer of brushwood is placed, and then a layer of thin plaster is spread on top of that, formed in such a way as to create a cylindrical dome. When the latter has dried another layer is poured on top, this time 20-25cm in thickness and containing Theran earth. Around 20 days later, the wooden moulding and the layer of thin plaster are removed, and another layer of plaster is added externally to enable more effective rainwater run-off. Since water is a valuable commodity, both the domes and the flat roofs constitute a system for collecting rainwater that is channelled to the underground cisterns.

town houses whose form has developed over the course of centuries, the mansion type of house must have developed during the 19th century. The older mansions located within the 'castles' would have had more in common with popular folk architecture, but there are very few intact examples left (one in Pyrgos and one in Emborio). The type that has survived to this day, for example in Frangomakala in Fira (the house of the descendants of the Latins) and mainly in Oia (captains' houses), does not exhibit the neoclassical elements that were predominant in the rest of Greece in that period. The origin of such mansions is probably Italian with Renaissance elements, but there is no absence of local influences. Their bulk is imposing and monolithic, in contrast to that of the ordinary houses. Their facades are monumental, often embellished with red stone and divided into vertical lines by pilasters which protrude a little from the surface of the wall. The door and windows are arranged symmetrically, but above the latter there are semicircular or round openings which emphasis the western origin of the building type.

Captains' houses in Oia and Pyrgos.

A little alleyway in Frangomakala, Fira.

CASTELLI

Fortified settlements ('kastelia')

In the 17th century, there were five 'kastelia' ('castles') or fortified settlements on Santorini. The most important, Kastro, was located on Skaros rock and constituted the seat of the Frankish occupiers, then came Ayios Nikolaos (modern Oia). The other three were located in the south of the island at Pyrgos, Emborio, and Akrotiri.

It is presumed that the first fortified settlements were created during the 14th century on Skaros and at Ayios Nikolaos. The whole population lived within the walls, in houses which had flat roofs like the central tower. The 'goulas' defensive towers of several storeys, remains of which are preserved in Emborio, Oia, Fira and Imerovigli, were also roofed; for reasons of security the floors with the ramparts and embrasures were accessed by ladders.

The system of defences of the time also consisted of watch towers - round constructions near the shores from which the movement of ships could be observed. Remains of these watch towers can be seen in Imerovigli and in the place called Vigla in the southern part of the island.

The castle at Ayios Nikolaos in Oia draws a multitude of people every superb sunset, to watch the sun go down.

Marble fragments in the stairway of the 'kasteli' of Pyrgos.

The fortified settlement of Skaros. (Thomas Hope, 1769-1831).

LOCAL CUISINE

Santorini offers the visitor a large variety of restaurants catering for all tastes and all pockets. In many of them, you can try local dishes such as the delicious fava - lentils, now rarely ground with a hand-mill - combined with a number of ingredients including onions or pieces of pork, and also served in soup or with aubergines and tomatoes. There are tomato fritters, fried or roasted white aubergines, 'bantada' (pieces of fried salted cod swathed in a smooth, creamy tomato sauce with slices of garlic and roasted in the oven), and stuffed, round courgettes. There are also 'melitinia', pastries made with myzithra and mastic which are offered at festivals, betrothals and also at any other happy occasion, and 'koufeto', the particular sweet consumed at weddings, made with almonds and honey.

And a meal has to be accompanied by one of the excellent wines of the island!

The religious festivals

In contrast to what happens in many other parts of Greece, the religious festivals on Santorini begin in the morning after the church service. Adjacent to every chapel, which is normally in private ownership, there is a room where the owners prepare and offer a meal that varies in nature according to the particular saint to whom the church is dedicated. Naturally, the local wine flows freely, and that traditional duo - violin and laouto - is always on hand to play typical Cycladic music, giving the Christian festival a truly dionysiac atmosphere.

The caper, well-known to us all, is one of the most beautiful wild flowers of the Greek landscape. As on other islands, not only the buds are used to flavour dishes but also the leaves of the plant. The caper was aleady known during the Minoan period and constituted a favourite motif of the ceramic artists of the prehistoric settlement at Akrotiri.

EXCURSIONS

Santorini has a good, asphalt road network; thus by car or motorcycle - rented or owned - the visitor can enjoy sightseeing on the island. A bicycle is out of the question, unless you are an athlete, since the island is mountainous and the hypsometrical differences are considerable. A few walking excursions are recommended here for nature lovers, along the old traditional footpaths which have been partly restored in recent years.

Staring at the cruise ships from Skaros rock.

Fira - Oia

Undoubtedly the most beautiful walk is that from Fira to Oia along the rim of the caldera. The paved path begins from the cathedral in the Catholic neighbourhood of Fira. It runs towards Firostefani and Imerovigli and arrives at the castle on Skaros rock. Further on, the path becomes one with the asphalt road at one point and thereafter resumes its separate course. Here, at the place where the width of the island is at its narrowest, the view is to the sea on both sides of it. After the asphalt road, the path runs uphill to Mikros Profitis Ilias, a vantage point from which there is the best view of the caldera. If walking late in the afternoon, you will be able to marvel at one of the most breathtaking sunsets in the whole Aegean. The path continues on to Perivolos and then joins the central, marble-paved street of Oia. (Duration of the walk - about 3 hours).

Imerovigli - Skaros

From Imerovigli, a fine path with wide steps runs down the side of the caldera. At the beginning there is the church of Ayia Theodosia, protectoress of castles. The path descends to the foot of the huge monolithic mass of Skaros where there are the remains of a church which collapsed during the earthquake of 1956, then it encircles the rock and terminates at the picturesque

Left: The walk from Fira to Imerovigli offers vistas of unparalleled beauty.

Ayios Yeorgios Xechreostis. Such churches - real sculptures - are to be found all over the island.

Boats both small and large leave Athinion, the port of Santorini, and the little harbour of Fira, on trips to Therasia and the volcano.

chapel of Panayia Theoskepasti which clings to the western face of the rock. Alternatively, you can climb to the remains of the castle on the summit of Skaros, and enjoy the panoramic, all-round view from there.

Profitis Ilias - Ancient Thera

Another walking tour is from Profitis Ilias to Ancient Thera, then on along the path to descend either Kamari or to Perissa. Since the ascent to the top of Profitis Ilias is quite a long one, you could go up by vehicle and limit the actual walk to the descent. Care should be taken on the route, especially when a strong wind is blowing, since the path is unstable in places. At any rate, it is

not recommended for those who are afraid of heights. (Duration - around 2 hours).

Pyrgos - Akrotiri

The route from Pyrgos to Akrotiri is also of interest. From the starting-point to Emborio there is a calderimi (cobbled roadway), and then a footpath which leads through the vineyards and the tranquil agricultural landscape of the island. (Duration - around 3 hours).

Akrotiri - Faros

Finally, another walk, not on a footpath but along the asphalt road, is recommended for those who are interested in lighthouses. Beginning from the village of Akrotiri, after about an hours' walk you will come to the tip of the island where there is an imposing lighthouse. In particular, if you decide to walk there at night the sudden appearance of its illuminated bulk around a curve in the road will reward your efforts.

The lighthouse at Akrotiri

This is one of the best in the Greek network of lighthouses. Built in 1892 by the French company La Société Collas et Michel, it was originally diesel-powered. It underwent restoration in 1925. Its function was interrupted during the 2nd World War and resumed in 1945, when it was operated by a staff of four. At that time it emitted light every 30 seconds and was visible over 25 nautical miles. In 1983 electrification was introduced there, and since 1988 the lighthouse has functioned automatically, emitting light over a radius of 24 nautical miles.

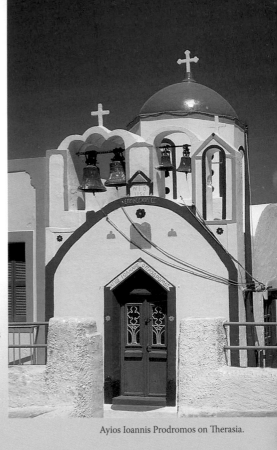

Ayios Ioannis Prodromos on Therasia.

BIBLIOGRAPHY

Ηρόδοτος IV
Πλάτων, Τίμαιος,
Πλάτων, Κριτίας
Ν. Platon, La civilisation égéenne II
Henri van Effenterre, Les Égéens
Nelly´s, Σαντορίνη 1925 -1930
Δ. Φιλιππίδης, Ελληνική παραδοσιακή αρχιτεκτονική, Σαντορίνη
Χρ. Ντούμας, Οι τοιχογραφίες της Θήρας, Αθήνα 1992
Χρ. Ντούμας, Σαντορίνη
Χρ. Ντούμας, Πρόσφατα ευρήματα από το Ακρωτήρι της Θήρας, Αθήνα 2000
Στ. Αλεξίου, Μινωικός πολιτισμός
Σπ. Μαρινάτος, Θησαυροί της Θήρας, Αθήνα 1972
Αλς, Περιοδική έκδοση της Εταιρείας Στήριξης Σπουδών Προϊστορικής Θήρας, τεύχη 1-5
Ελλάδα 1842-1885, Ιστορικά, τοπογραφικά και καλιτεχνικά ντοκουμέντα στα κύρια Αγγλικά περιοδικα. Αθήνα 1984 Εκδόσεις Α. Nicolas.